Pioneers of Space Law

Pioneers of Space Law

Edited by

Stephan Hobe

A publication of the
International Institute of Space Law

MARTINUS
NIJHOFF
PUBLISHERS

LEIDEN • BOSTON
2013

ISBN 978-90-04-24027-8 (hardback)
ISBN 978-90-04-24028-5 (e-book)

Koninklijke Brill NV incorporates the imprints BRILL, Global Oriental, Hotei Publishing, IDC Publishers and Martinus Nijhoff Publishers.

This book is printed on acid-free paper.

Table of Contents

Foreword

As is well known, international space law is less than 50 years old. Although the work for the codification of space law started in the late 1950s, shortly after the launching of the first artificial satellite Sputnik 1, the Outer Space Treaty was adopted only in January 1967. However, much earlier, even as early as 1932, the first ideas about legal rules for human activities in outer space were considered. Very little is known about these early drafts and proposals, such as the one of Vladimir Mandl in his famous treatise "Space law – a Problem of Space Flight" published in 1932 in German (Das Weltraumrecht – ein Problem der Raumfahrt). But also early pioneering works of other scholars are relatively unknown. Therefore in 2009, the International Institute of Space Law welcomed the initiative of its Directorate of Studies to publish a book about the "Pioneers of Space Law". It is worth mentioning in this respect, that – at least for the purposes of this book – a pioneer is an eminent scholar who made an original contribution to the science of space law. Some of them had already made considerable (pioneering) contributions to the field of air law, while others started genuinely in the space law field. Essentially, this book is a tribute to the memory of these pioneers, who are no longer among us.

The pioneers to be included in the book and the colleagues who would be asked to write about them were agreed by the Board of Directors of the International Institute of Space Law. Photographs of the pioneers were kindly arranged by the authors, and in most cases come from personal collections. The list of pioneers is by no means intended to be exhaustive, and others could be honoured in a second and further editions of this book.

We trust that this book will be welcomed not only by the community of space lawyers, but also beyond that, within the community of international lawyers as well as among historians and political scientists interested in the evolution of legal scholarship in the field of space activity. And of course we hope that especially the pioneers would not only have liked this idea, but would also have liked what has been written about them.

Tanja Masson-Zwaan
President, IISL

Stephan Hobe
Chairman, IISL Directorate of Studies

Chapter I **Alex Meyer** (15.12.1879 – 21.08.1978)

Stephan Hobe*

During his long life, Alex Meyer proudly achieved something which only very few other jurists have achieved. He became a pioneer of the science of air law as well as a pioneer of the science of space law.[1]

Alex Meyer was already 77 when the first artificial satellite Sputnik I was brought into outer space by the Soviet Union. At that time he could look back on a very successful career as an aviation lawyer.[2] His two seminal writings, one in 1908 on "The Legal Consequences of "Opening up" Air Space" (Die Erschließung des Luftraums und ihre rechtlichen Folgen) and the other, published in 1944 on "Freedom of the Air as a Legal Problem" (Freiheit der Luft

* Director of the Institute of Air and Space Law and Holder of the Chair for Public International Law, European and International Economic Law of the University of Cologne.

1 *See* Stephan Hobe, *Vladimir Mandl, Alex Meyer, Welf-Heinrich Prince of Hanover, Friedrich-Wilhelm von Rauchhaupt – Early Writings in German on the Young Discipline of Space Law, in* PROCEEDINGS OF THE 50TH COLLOQUIUM ON THE LAW OF OUTER SPACE, PRAGUE 2010, 21 *et seq*, 23-25 (AIAA, 2011).

2 *See* the *liber amicorum* in his honor which gives an impression of his influence and his writings, MANFRED BODENSCHATZ & KARL-HEINZ BÖCKSTIEGEL & PETER WEIDES (EDS.), FESTSCHRIFT FÜR ALEX MEYER (LIBER AMICORUM FOR ALEX MEYER) (1975). On the occasion of his 80th anniversary he received a book with his selected writings, ALEX MEYER, LUFTRECHT IN FÜNF JAHRZEHNTEN (AIR LAW IN FIVE DECADES) (1961), with an Avant Propos of the then Federal Transport Minister of Germany Dr. Hans-Christoph Seebohm.

Stephan Hobe (ed.), Pioneers of Space Law
 ISBN *978-90-04-24027-8. pp. 5-18*

als Rechtsproblem), many dogmatically inspiring articles on the matter of air law,[3] as well as numerous memberships and an active position in the German and international aviation law community had made Meyer a renowned personality in this field on the national and international plane. But as we will show in the following the merits of this great man did not stop with the description of developments in the area of air law. From the very early times on Alex Meyer was aware of new developments of man leaving the Earth and the Earth' atmosphere and reaching outer space. And what he had to contribute was quite remarkable. It is therefore very well justified to rank him among the pioneers of space law. In the following we will first briefly sketch out the biography of Alex Meyer before his contribution to the science of space law will be outlined. This will allow for a conclusion in which we will point out the particular merits of this scholar for the science of space law.

A. Biography[4]

Alexis Moritz Philipp Meyer was born on 15 December 1879 as a son of a Prussian civil servant in Berlin. His first encounter with the Cologne region was when he visited High School in Cologne and Elberfeld, a city today belonging to Wuppertal, which is a 400.000 citizen city in the vicinity of Cologne. Later on Alex Meyer studied law in Geneva, Munich, Berlin and Bonn. He passed the first juridicial state examination in Cologne in 1902 with a notable mark and the second examination in 1907 in Berlin. Before, he had already successfully completed his doctorate in Leipzig on the civil law topic of "Notion and Protection of Credits according to German Civil Law". In 1913 and until 1914 Alex Meyer became a judge in Szechin (formerly Stettin, belonging at that time to East Prussia and today a city in Poland). During the First World War from 1914 to 1917 Alex Meyer served in the German Army. From

3 *See* the bibliography assembled by Hans Pick which covers 298 entries at pp. 457-482 of the *liber amicorum*; the works specifically on space law are listed at the end of this chapter.

4 For biographical notes about Alex Meyer *see* Horst Bittlinger & Marietta Benkö, Institute of Air and Space Law 1925 – 2005, 12 *et seq.* (2005); reference is also made to the *curriculum vitae* of Alex Meyer in the archives of the Faculty of Law of the University of Cologne.

1917 until 1918 he worked in the civil administration of Flanders, Brussels. Between 1918 and 1920 Alex Meyer worked in the Federal Ministry for Food and Agriculture. In 1920 he became a civil servant in Koblenz and between 1923 and 1933 worked in the Chancellery of the Reich in Berlin, respectively between 1929 and 1933 in the higher administration (Oberpräsidium) of the Province Brandenburg. From 1933 to 1936 Meyer worked for the Prussian government in Düsseldorf as legal advisor but, due to his Jewish belief ,was forced to retire from this post.

The next step of Meyer's professional career is somewhat left in the dark. The uncontested fact is that in 1938 he received a call from New York University to teach Air Law. Whether there was some contribution from the German authorities who because of Meyer's Jewish background did not grant him the visa for the U.S., or for another reason: the curriculum vitae at the Faculty of Law of Cologne University makes it clear that the outbreak of the Second World War made the acceptance of this temporary professorship impossible.

As a consequence Meyer left Germany in 1939 for Zurich, Switzerland. Here, in Switzerland, Meyer survived the Second World War. After the war he was rehabilitated in 1953 when the injury suffered from his forced retirement in 1938 was officially recognized as unjust and when he was put with retroactive effect as of April 1, 1939 at a specifically high post in the German administration.

After the war, in 1950 Alex Meyer returned to Cologne and started to teach air law at the University of Cologne as of 1950. In 1951 he initiated the re-opening of the Institute of Air Law which had been founded in 1925 by Professor Otto Schreiber in Kaliningrad (Königsberg) as the first research unit of its type. The Institute did not exist any more – it was destroyed where it was situated last, *i.e.* at Leipziger Platz in the center of Berlin. Before, the Institute had moved from Königsberg (Kaliningrad) to Leipzig during the period of 1929 to 1939 and then from 1939 to 1945 had its place in Berlin.[5]

Directors after the early death of Otto Schreiber were Hans Oppikofer in Leipzig and Rüdiger Schleicher in Berlin.[6] After the complete destruction of the Institute in 1945 it did not exist until Meyer started to revive it in 1951.

5 *See* Bittlinger & Benkö, *supra* note 4, at 1-10.

6 On Rüdiger Schleicher *see* Stephan Hobe, *In Memoriam Rüdiger Schleicher – Eine Erinnerung an das Wirken des dritten Direktors des Instituts für Luftrecht*, 59 Zeitschrift für Luft- und Weltraumrecht, 1-17 (2010).

The Institute's research work after the Second World War had started as a research facility for air law in 1951. Later on, it was re-named "Institute for Air Law and Questions of Space Law". Already in 1952 Alex Meyer started to edit again a German Journal for Air (and Space as of 1959) Law (Zeitschrift für Luft- [und Weltraum]recht) which he felt to be in the tradition of the old "Archive of Air Law" (Archiv des Luftrechts) that was edited by the Institute from 1931 until 1943. Meyer was appointed Honorary Professor at the University of Cologne in 1953 and taught air law at this University until 1974. He was active as the president of the Legal Committee of the Council of the Federal Ministry of Traffic, the Legal Committee of the German Society of Air Law, as well as the Air and Space Law Committee of the German Group of the International Law Association. Moreover, Meyer was a member of the Air Transport Commission of the International Chamber of Commerce, of the American Society of International Law and the Instituto de Derecho Aeronáutico y Interplanetario in Buenos Aires.

Alex Meyer published approximately 300 books and articles of which 28 publications are devoted to space law; these publications are listed at the end of this chapter[7] whereas the oeuvre in air law is documented *supra*.[8]

B. Alex Meyer's Importance for the Development of Space Law

With his 28 publications Alex Meyer added a considerable contribution also to the discipline of space law. Almost all of his articles deal with rather general questions on the legal status of outer space and of the celestial bodies, enriched by articles on the military uses of outer space and the problem of space warfare as well as the question of the applicability of humanitarian international law to outer space activities.

Basically, the main ideas were developed in an article of a very early time, *i.e.* in a paper read at the Third International Astronautical Congress (IAC) in Stuttgart on September 5, 1952. This was early insofar as it was, first of all, before the modern part of space flight started (there were of course some attempts during World War II by Germany, mainly the product of the

7 *See* section D below.

8 *See supra* note 3.

engineering of Herman Oberth and Wernher von Braun[9]) on October 4, 1957 by the launch of Sputnik I. Moreover, it took a while before the international community started to draft legal rules in the late 1950s and early 1960s. It is well justified to highlight what Alex Meyer had to say whereby he greatly profited from his deep and profound knowledge of the science of air law. We can find very interesting ideas of a scientist who despite his advanced age still participated very actively in the intellectual discourse of his science and delivered a very substantive contribution. In the following Meyer's main ideas shall be briefly summarized:

1. *No Need in Space Law for an Analogy to Air Law, to the Law of the Sea or of Antarctica*

It is striking that Meyer was very determined to not allow at all any analogy of this new area of outer space law, neither to air law, nor to the law of the sea. In his opinion outer space would in fact be completely different. It would be very distinct in nature – such was the conviction of Alex Meyer. In other words: it was the fundamentally different structure of the sovereignty of free outer space that would not allow for any analogy. This highlights in a significant way that Meyer had at that early time already the distinct understanding that no rights of sovereignty could and should govern outer space. Rather this new medium for human activities would and should be free of any sovereign rights of states.[10] Of course, also questions of demarcation were addressed in depth.

2. *The Question of Delimitation of Air and Outer Space*

Whereas at the beginning Meyer pleaded in favor of a boundary at approximately 200 to 300 kilometers above sea level as the boundary between air and outer space,[11] he later corrected this view by describing the provisions of

9 *See* more recently on Wernher von Braun the book of Stefan Brauburger, Wernher von Braun (2009).

10 Alex Meyer, *Rechtliche Probleme des Weltraumfluges*, 2 Zeitschrift für Luftrecht, 34 (1953).

11 *Id.*

the Outer Space Treaty. At that time he concluded that the von Karman line at about 80 kilometers above sea level would be an appropriate possibility for delimitation.[12] Other questions associated to this very important problem were, on the one hand, that the Chicago Convention on international air transport would, of course, remain in force and would make evident its full importance.[13] Moreover, closely connected to problems derived from the Chicago Convention, Meyer insisted that there was no right to fly over foreign territory without an explicit permission when conducting space flight.[14] It is well known that this question is not settled yet in international space law.[15] Even 50 years after Alex Meyer's writing it is unclear, due to a lack of State practice, which legal regime may govern here. Some authors plead for an inclusion of this right of overflight into the freedom of outer space, others negate this possibility with reasons not far away from the ones found by Alex Meyer in the 1950s.[16]

3. *The Dispute of the Approach to Delimitation*

And with regard to the delimitation question, Meyer involved himself in a doctrinal dispute. On the one hand, other famous air lawyers like Chaumont in his book on "The Law of Outer Space" ("Le droit de l'espace") as well as Quadri in his Hague Academy lecture entitled "International Space Law"

12 Alex Meyer, *Der Weltraumvertrag,* 16 Zeitschrift für Luftrecht und Weltraumrechtsfragen, 65-77 (1967).

13 Alex Meyer, *Die Staatshoheit im Luftraum und die Entwicklungen im Weltraumrecht,* 14 Zeitschrift für Luftrecht und Weltraumrechtsfragen, 296 (1965).

14 *Id.*

15 *See* on that problem *inter alia* Stephan Hobe, *Is there a right through foreign airspace, in* Space Law and Policy – Summer Course: Basic Materials, 89 *et seq.* (ECSL ed., 1994).

16 *See* for an overview Walter Schwenk, *Die Bedeutung des Luftrechts für Weltraumtätigkeiten (The Importance of Air Law for Outer Space Activities), in* Handbuch des Weltraumrechts, 135, 141 *et seq.* (Karl-Heinz Böckstiegel ed., 1991); Stephan Hobe, *supra* note 15, *passim.*

("Droit International Cosmique")[17] had vigorously pleaded for the so-called functional approach.[18] This approach would not fix a (rather artificial) boundary and link to it the delimitation between air space and outer space but would decide the question of the applicability of air law or space law according to the function of the respective vehicle.[19] If the eventual aim would include outer space, space law would be applicable whereas in the opposite case air law would be applicable.

Meyer did not subscribe to this functional approach. Rather he explicitly expressed his uneasiness about the treatment of air space and outer space being subject to one single legal order. This unity would not be justified, neither from a physicists point of view, nor would it be the appropriate legal designation.[20]

For Alex Meyer it was clear as early as 1962 that the delimitation of air space and outer space required an international agreement sponsored by the United Nations in which all states had consented on such delimitation of air space and outer space.[21] With regard to such an agreement one must say that even more than 50 years after Alex Meyer's writings we are not very close to arriving at such an international agreement.

4. *A Contiguous Zone between Air and Outer Space?*

Another doctrinal dispute was the one with McGill's Institute of Air and Space Law's first Director John Cobb Cooper on the existence of a contiguous zone between air space and outer space comparable to the contiguous zone between the coastal state and the High Seas. Whereas Cooper had vehement-

17 Charles Chaumont, Le droit de l'espace (1960) and Roland Quadri, *Droit international cosmique, in* Recueil des cours (1959) III, 510 *et seq.*

18 Charles Chaumont, *supra* note 17, at 52 and Quadri, *supra* note 17, at 553, 561, 579.

19 Alex Meyer, *Die Bedeutung der Festsetzung einer Grenze zwischen Luftraum und Weltraumgebiet (The Importance to Fix a Boundary Between Air and Outer Space)*, 11 Zeitschrift für Luftrecht und Weltraumrechtsfragen, 106, 112 *et seq.* (1962).

20 This is particularly stressed and extensively argued by Meyer in the just quoted article on the importance of the possibility to fix a boundary between air and outer space, *supra* note 19, 114 *et seq.*

21 *See* Meyer, *supra* note 19, at 106, 116.

ly pleaded for such existence, Meyer simply denies the possibility to draw any kind of such analogy to the law of the sea. He justifies his opinion because of the non-existence of any sovereign rights in outer space as opposed to the delimitation of the land and the territorial waters towards the high seas.[22] And in fact: looking at this problem in a current perspective, *i.e.* more than 50 years later, one cannot but agree with the arguments of Alex Meyer. Neither treaty law nor the practice of States have given rise to the assumption of any existence of such a contiguous zone between air and outer space.

5. *The Placement of Space Stations*

Moreover, in Meyer's view there were no problems to allow any kind of placement of space stations in outer space.[23] This was, of course, not anything of current use at the time of Meyer's writings but was realized later for example with Saljut or Mir from the then Soviet Union or Skylab and most prominently with the International Space Station Freedom. The statement at the time of Meyer's writings did not yet involve the complicated question of, on the one hand, a preservation of jurisdictional rights of the launching state over the station – they were explicitly excluded from Meyer's considerations,[24] – nor, on the other hand, questions of the selective legal regime for the space stations tackled. These problems were, of course, later on dealt with in Art. VIII of the Outer Space Treaty of 1967 and, moreover, in the famous Space Station Agreements of 1988 and 1998.[25] But more importantly at the time of

22 Alex Meyer, *Kritische Bemerkungen zu neueren Erörterungen über die Rechtsprobleme des Weltraums (Critical Remarks on Recent Discussions concerning Legal Problems of Outer Space)* 7 Zeitschrift für Luftrecht, 194, 204 (1958).

23 Alex Meyer, *Rechtsprobleme des Weltraumgebietes, in* Raketentechnik und Raumfahrtforschung, 1, 6 (1960).

24 *Id.*

25 Agreement Among the Government of Canada, the Governments of ESA Member States, the Government of Japan, the Russian Federation and the United States Concerning Cooperation on the Civil International Space Station, of January 29, 1998, reprinted in Space Law Basic Legal Documents, D.II.4.1 (Karl-Heinz Böckstiegel & Marietta Benkö & Stephan Hobe eds., 2011).

Meyer's writing was, again, his absolute openness for new legal questions, arising from human endeavors in outer space.

6. *On the Legal Regulation of Military Uses of Outer Space*

With regard to military uses of outer space Meyer had very clearly reflected the ambiguous character of space technology and the danger of a further militarization of outer space in view of the eminent interests of the major space powers in the 1960s and 1970s.[26] He heavily criticized the fact that the Outer Space Treaty speaks of peaceful purposes but never defines what really must be understood as "peaceful". Whereas his personal hope was, on the one hand, at the end of the day to be able to understand "peaceful" in a sense going beyond "non-aggressive", Meyer, on the other hand, was very realistic and saw that the practice mainly of the super powers would not allow to give "peaceful" an understanding of "non-military" but rather of "non-aggressive". This realistic perspective was made clear in his assessment of Art. IV of the Outer Space Treaty as well as with regard to some considerations of Alex Meyer on humanitarian law.[27] With regard to using outer space and the military purposes and applying humanitarian law, he had to highlight some difficulty stemming from the fact that outer space, through its special legal character, had not been designed for containing such important notions as the notion of "neutrality" in the humanitarian legal sense.[28] These questions belong to the most interesting and new questions discussed among space lawyers and specialists from international humanitarian law.

26 This is shown especially in his article *„Die Auslegung des Begriffs „friedlich" im Lichte des Weltraumvertrages" (The Interpretation of the Term "Peaceful" in the Light of the Space Treaty)*, 18 ZEITSCHRIFT FÜR LUFTRECHT UND WELTRAUMRECHTSFRAGEN, 28 *et seq.* (1969).

27 Alex Meyer, *The term "peaceful" in the Light of the Treaty on Principles Governing the Activities of States in the Exploration and Use of Outer Space, including the Moon and other Celestial Bodies*, 17 ZEITSCHRIFT FÜR LUFTRECHT UND WELTRAUMRECHTSFRAGEN, 110 *et seq.* (1968).

28 Alex Meyer, *Exploration of Outer Space and Neutrality, in* PROCEEDINGS OF THE 4TH COLLOQUIUM ON THE LAW OF OUTER SPACE, WASHINGTON D.C. 1961, 244 *et seq.* (1963).

C. Conclusion

What is the essence of the space law oeuvre of Alex Meyer? Why is it justified to award to him the unofficial title of "pioneer" of space law? A pioneer, by the way, who introduced space law to the German Journal of Air and Space Law in 1952 by quoting one of the really first pioneers of space law, Vladimir Mandl,[29] who in 1932 had concluded that the comprehensive reflection about a legal problem of and in outer space would tremendously contribute to the solution of the problem.[30]

I believe it is well justified to list Alex Meyer among the pioneers of space law because he had started his legal observations long before space law was written down and even before modern space flights had commenced. The important fact here is that – probably due to his longstanding occupation with the other pioneering science of air law which he had accompanied from its early days on – especially by making contributions as early as 1908,[31] Meyer had a lot of experience and a lot of reference material at hand that allowed him to draw comparisons and decide where new legal ground had to be paved. Moreover, Alex Meyer as a man in his seventies first formulated the newly emerging rules and then vehemently pleaded for the legal codification of such rules. His early writings in 1952 basically paved the way for an understanding that would allow human activities in outer space but would surround this freedom by a legal frame. Among Meyer's key points we find of course the question of the legal status of outer space, the delimitation question, problems of definitions in space legal science as the basic notions of space law and the ever-lasting question of an appropriate interpretation of the meaning of "peaceful" in Art. IV of the Outer Space Treaty.

With all these writings Alex Meyer did not only open legal avenues which later on – from 1967 to 1979 – became included in the five international conventions. As was demonstrated, Meyer also basically paved the way for

29 Alex Meyer, *Weltraumrecht*, 1 Zeitschrift für Luftrecht, 234 (1952).

30 Vladimir Mandl, Space Law – A Problem of Space Flight (Das Weltraumrecht – ein Problem der Raumfahrt) 14 (1932).

31 In this year, 11 years before the famous Paris Convention of 1919 came into existence, Meyer wrote a booklet on The Conquering of Air Space and its Legal Consequences (Die Erschliessung des Luftraums in ihren rechtlichen Folgen) (1908).

the doctrinal discussion of the current problems. And as can be seen, even 60 years after his initial work with respect to many problems we still discuss a great number of similar questions.

D. Selected Bibliography

The articles of Alex Meyer on space law include:

(1) *Weltraumrecht (Space Law)*, 1 ZEITSCHRIFT FÜR LUFTRECHT, 234 – 236 (1952)

(2) *Rechtliche Probleme des Weltraumfluges*, 2 ZEITSCHRIFT FÜR LUFTRECHT, 31 – 43 (1953)

(3) *Legal Problems of Flight into Outer Space*, LEGAL PROBLEMS OF SPACE EXPLORATION, 1961, 8 – 19;

(4) *Anmerkungen zu einem Beitrag von J.C. Cooper*, 5 ZEITSCHRIFT FÜR LUFTRECHT, 180 *et seq.* (1956)

(5) *Der künstliche Erdsatellit als Rechtsproblem*, NEUE ZÜRCHER ZEITUNG , 22 October 1957, at 2

(6)*Kritische Bemerkungen zu neueren Erörterungen über „Rechtliche Probleme des Weltraums“*, 7 ZEITSCHRIFT FÜR LUFTRECHT, 194 – 207 (1958)

(7) *Rechtsprobleme des Weltraumgebiets*, *in* LUFT- UND WELTRAUMRECHTLICHE GEGENWARTSFRAGEN (Riese/Meyer eds., 1958)

(8) *Die Rechtsprobleme des Weltraums*, AUSSENPOLITIK, 645 – 653 (1959)

(9) *Behandlung der Rechtsprobleme des Weltraums durch die Vereinten Nationen (UNO)*, 8 ZEITSCHRIFT FÜR LUFTRECHT, 261 – 264 (1959)

(10) *Some Problems relating to Space Law*, *in* PROCEEDINGS OF THE 2nd COLLOQUIUM ON THE LAW OF OUTER SPACE, LONDON 1959, 120 – 122 (1960)

(11) *Recht im Weltraum*, 9 ZEITSCHRIFT FÜR LUFTRECHT UND WELTRAUMRECHTSFRAGEN, 209 – 214 (1960)

(12) *Legal Problems of Outer Space*, *in* US COMMITTEE AERONAUTICAL AND SPACE SCIENCES, 500 – 510 (1961)

(13) *Exploration of Outer Space and Neutrality, in* PROCEEDINGS OF THE 4th COLLOQUIUM ON THE LAW OF OUTER SPACE, WASHINGTON D.C. 1961, 244 – 257 (1963)

(14) *Die Bedeutung der Festsetzung einer Grenze zwischen Luftraum und Weltraumgebiet,* 11 ZEITSCHRIFT FÜR LUFTRECHT UND WELTRAUMRECHTSFRAGEN, 106 – 121 (1962)

(15) *Die Raumfahrt als Ursache rechtlicher Probleme, in*: RAUMFAHRT WOHIN?, 166-179 (1962)

(16) WIRKLICHKEIT UND NOTWENDIGKEIT DER STAATSHOHEIT IM LUFTRAUM UND FREIHEIT DES WELTRAUMGEBIETES, 12 ZEITSCHRIFT FÜR LUFTRECHT UND WELTRAUMRECHTSFRAGEN, 2– 11 (1963)

(17) *Behandlung der Rechtsprobleme des Weltraums durch die Vereinten Nationen (UN) seit 1959*, 12 ZEITSCHRIFT FÜR LUFTRECHT UND WELTRAUMRECHTSFRAGEN, 207 – 213 (1963)

(18) *Über den gegenwärtigen Stand des Weltraumrechts, in* NJW 1963, 193

(19) Alex Meyer, *Rechtsprobleme der Luft- und Raumfahrt, in* JAHRBUCH DER WISSENSCHAFTLICHEN GESELLSCHAFT FÜR LUFT- UND RAUMFAHRT, 109-115 (1964)

(20) *Die Staatshoheit im Luftraum und die Entwicklungen im Weltraum,* 14 ZEITSCHRIFT FÜR LUFTRECHT UND WELTRAUMRECHTSFRAGEN, 296 – 311 (1965)

(21) *Das Weltraumrecht und die Staaten – Betrachtungen zu dem gleichnamigen Buch von Andrew G. Haley,* 14 ZEITSCHRIFT FÜR LUFTRECHT UND WELTRAUMRECHTSFRAGEN, 2-43 (1965)

(22) *Die Auslegung des Begriffs „friedlich" im Hinblick auf die von Präsident Johnson angekündigte Schaffung von bemannten Raumstationen „Military Manned Orbiting Laboratories (MOLS)"*, 15 ZEITSCHRIFT FÜR LUFTRECHT UND WELTRAUMRECHTSFRAGEN, 36 – 39 (1966)

(23) *Straftaten im Weltraum, in* JAHRBUCH DER RECHTSWISSENSCHAFTLICHEN FAKULTÄT DER UNIVERSITÄT THESSALONIKI, 219 – 238 (1966)

(24) *Der Weltraumvertrag,* 16 ZEITSCHRIFT FÜR LUFTRECHT UND WELTRAUMRECHTSFRAGEN, 65 – 77 (1967)

(25) *Der Begriff „friedlich" im Lichte des Weltraumvertrages,* 17 ZEITSCHRIFT FÜR LUFTRECHT UND WELTRAUMRECHTSFRAGEN, 110 – 119 (1968)

(26) *Rechtsprobleme des Weltraums,* 18 ZEITSCHRIFT FÜR LUFTRECHT UND WELTRAUMRECHTSFRAGEN, 10 – 39 (1969)

(27) *Rechtsprobleme der Mondlandung,* 18 ZEITSCHRIFT FÜR LUFTRECHT UND WELTRAUMRECHTSFRAGEN, 203 – 204 (1969)

(28) *Rückschau auf Luftrecht und Weltraumrecht – An Stelle einer Abschiedsvorlesung,* 23 ZEITSCHRIFT FÜR LUFTRECHT UND WELTRAUMRECHTSFRAGEN, 228 – 241 (1974)

Chapter II **Eugène Pépin** (27.06.1887 – 27.04.1988)

Armel Kerrest*

Professor Eugène Pépin was born on June 27th, 1887; he died on April 27th 1988. Professor Pépin thus lived during the hundred years which saw the birth of aviation and the first man on the moon. He was already 16 years old when, in 1903, the brothers Wright made the first air flight. He was 82 when in 1969 Neil Armstrong and Buzz Aldrin walked on the moon. At that time, he was still very active and stayed active during the following 18 years. We have the impression that time does not pass the same way for Eugène Pépin as for other human beings. He had already known a rich career when in 1928, at the age of 50, he got married. He continued teaching until 1982 at the Institute of Studies of International Relations in Paris (Institut d'études des relations internationales contemporaines). Back then he was already 95 years old. During his centenary in 1987, he still displayed an incredible "youth" since he gave speeches at the general meeting of ICAO and for students of the Institute of Air and Space Law of the University of McGill. Professor Pépin was more involved in air law than in space law but he foresaw the evolution of space law very accurately and took an important part in its development. He has thus an indisputable place in this book on "pioneers" of space law.

* Full professor at the University of Western Brittany.
The author would like to thank Mr. Pépin's son, Mr. Henry Pépin, Michel et Danielle Bourely, Tanja Masson-Zwaan (IISL), Ram Jakhu and Ari Munisami (McGill-University), Didier Lecoq (Club d'Aviation de Touraine), Ambassador Michel Wachenheim and Mr. Denis Wibaux (ICAO) for the precious information given.

Stephan Hobe (ed.), Pioneers of Space Law

ISBN 978-90-04-24027-8. pp. 21-32

He did not only enjoy a very long life but his life was extraordinarily complete and rich, too. Eugène Pépin intervened not only in the domains of air and space law but he also showed a large eclecticism and an extraordinary intellectual curiosity.

Before presenting all his achievements, let us examine the numerous stages of his life.

A Biography

He was born in 1887; his father was an auctioneer[1] in Chinon and shaped his interest in pleasant things and art. He studied in Chinon at the Rabelais secondary school and got his baccalaureat in 1904 in the section of mathematics. He then had a brilliant high education in Paris: the school of High Commercial Studies (*Hautes Études Commerciales*, HEC), then *License ès lettres, License* in law. He then wrote a doctoral thesis in history of law on "High and low forests of Chinon"[2] which was published in 1911. In 1905 he wrote another thesis in law on the British Aliens Act of 1905: "The issue of foreigners in England".[3] This brilliant work was written under the direction of the well known professor Louis Renault of the Paris law faculty. This text was published in 1913 with a very laudatory preface of Louis Renault.

After this unusual multidisciplinary training, Eugène Pépin was recruited in 1910 as Secretary of the President of the first International Air Navigation Conference. This drove Mr. Pépin towards aircraft activity and its laws and rules, a field where he was recognized as one of the best specialists later.

In 1913, he became a member of the French Society of International Law[4] and of the Society of Comparative Law.[5]

During the First World War, as a lieutenant and later as a captain, he could use his knowledge in the field of air activities. He was appointed as the leader of one out of eight sections of air photography of the French armies.

1 A so-called *commissaire priseur.*

2 *Les Haute et Basse forets de Chinon.*

3 *La question des étrangers en Angleterre.*

4 *Société française pour le droit international, SFDI.*

5 *Société française de droit comparé.*

From 1917 on he worked in cooperation with the American Forces of General Pershing. Particularly he was an instructor for the American recruits for air photography. In 1920, he was honoured by being given the cross of knight of the Legion of Honour for his military activities in gratitude for these actions.

After the war, he was transferred from the ministry of defence to the ministry of Foreign Affairs and participated in the Versailles Peace Conference as Secretary of the Central Drafting Committee of the Conference. He was held responsible for preparing the final text of the Peace Treaties. In January 1920 he was put in charge of the publication of the documents of the Conference. This difficult and long work was achieved in 1934.

In consideration of his particular skills, he was also a member of the Committee of Geography which was held responsible for defining the borders of the new States created by the treaty. He also participated in the work of the Aeronautical Commission created for preparing the Paris Conference on air navigation of 1919 and the Convention on International Civil Aviation as its result.

From 1920 until 1930, Eugène Pépin was the head of the juridical, economic and financial section of the Service of the League of Nations in the French Ministry of Foreign Affairs. He participated at the annual conferences of the Organisation and at the meetings of the Council. He was part of the French delegation in several international conferences organized in this framework, e.g. conferences on traffic of opium, exploitation of women, arms trade, ammunitions and military materials. In 1930 he took part in the first Conference for the Codification of International Law.

In 1929 Pépin was nominated to become deputy legal adviser to the Ministry of Foreign Affairs.

The pursuance of his career led him to be interested in Latin America. From 1925 until 1930 he was the agent of the French government before the Franco-Mexican Arbitration Commission for the settlement of disputes related to damages inflicted on French citizens in Mexico during the Mexican revolutions.[6] He kept a great interest in this country and South America in

6 Eugene Pépin, La réparation des dommages causés aux étrangers par des mouvements révolutionnaires, jurisprudence de la Commission Franco-Mexicaine des réclamations 249 (1933) *available at* :http://gallica.bnf.fr/ark:/12148/bpt6k5500229c.r=p%C3%A9pin.langDE.

general, for its culture and its art. He gathered an important collection of art objects.[7] In 1928 he attended the VI. Pan-American Conference of Havana.

His interest in air law led him to participate in the Legal Sub-Committee of the International Commission for Air Navigation (ICAN) from 1922 on (*Commission Internationale de la Navigation aérienne*) (C.I.N.A).[8]

In 1930 Eugène Pépin became a legal adviser to the Japanese Ministry of Foreign Affairs; he remained in this function until 1933 when Japan left SDN. He participated in the works of the Investigating Committee of the League of Nations (Lytton Commission) on the differences between China and Japan about Manchuria. He then stayed in the Far East for the French Ministry of Foreign Affairs to study the problems of Pacific and South East Asia (Philippines, Indonesia, Malaysia, Indochina Thailand and India). He represented France to the South Pacific Commission.

In 1934 he studied how to teach French in Latin America. During a period of five years, from 1934 to 1939, he was especially in charge of Latin America in the French Ministry of Foreign Affairs and worked on the publication of scientific works.

The Second World War led him back to air issues. In 1939 and 1940, he was appointed to the General Headquarters of the French armies where he was in charge of the air photographs for the Headquarters of the Commander-in-Chief. From 1940 till 1944 he was the head of the economic section of the services of the armistice and later its principal private secretary to the director. During this period, he cooperated with the Army Resistance Organization.

In 1945 Eugène Pépin began his Canadian career by being appointed to be the head of the Legal Studies Section for Air Transportation, in the provisional International Civil Aviation Organisation in Montreal. Quite naturally he became the director of the legal bureau of the permanent organization when on April 4th, 1947 the Chicago Convention came into force. He assumed

7 He possessed, for instance, a rather enigmatic peace of art, a crystal scull which is known as "Crane Pépin", the origin of which is disputed, *available at:* http://mot-scles.lemondeprecolombien.com/index_90.htm, www.binoche-renaud-giquello.com/flash/index.jsp?id=9738&idCp=33&lng=fr lot n°131.

8 International Commission for Air Navigation (ICAN).
Commission Internationale de la Navigation aérienne created in 1919, established in 1922.

this function until 1953 when, at the age of 66, he was affected by the age limit even though he would have accomplished so many more things afterwards. Once again, time and age do not have the same significance for Eugène Pépin as for other human beings.

After retiring from ICAO, he stayed in Montreal in order to take the directorship of the Institute of Air and Space Law at McGill University. He was professor from 1951 to 1953 and was its director from 1955 to 1959. Already interested into space activities, he obtained from the Board of Governors of McGill University the change of the title of the Institute into "Institute of Air and Space Law".

In 1961, when he was already far beyond the age of retirement for a "normal" human being, he started a new career as a professor of the Paris Institute for Studies of International Relations (*Institut d'études des relations internationales* (ILERI)). This Institute was created by Professor René Cassin, Peace Nobel Price winner. Eugène Pépin taught there until 1982. At that time, he was 95 years old!

After his return to France, Eugène Pépin went closer to his native Touraine which he still felt connected to. He intervened particularly in order to support the restoration of his home town Chinon. He worked for the creation of a safeguarded area in the old centre of the city. In 1970 he accepted the presidency of the archaeological society of Touraine. He wrote numerous books and articles on this beautiful region.[9]

During his centenary in 1987, he was celebrated by many, particularly by the OACI and McGill Institutes of Air and Space Law.[10] He died in 1988 as if, still in good physical and moral condition, he was bowing out discreetly discretely after such a remarkable life.

B Activities of Eugène Pépin in the Field of Air Law

Eugène Pépin was present in person from the very beginning of the development of air law on since he participated in the first International Air Navigation Conference of Paris in 1910 by assisting the secretary of its President. He also attended the following conference in 1919 where the le-

9 Eugene Pépin, Histoire de Touraine (1935).

10 Gennady P. Zhukov, *In honor of Eugène Pépin*, 16 Journal of Space Law 1 (1988).

gal nature of airspace was decided upon. He took part in the Commission in charge of drafting the text of the 1919 Paris Convention on air navigation.

Even though he assumed other functions in the diplomatic domain in France, Mexico or Japan, he remained in contact with air law by being a member of the Legal Sub-Committee of the International Commission for Air Navigation since 1922.

From 1945 to 1947, Eugène Pépin was the head of the legal studies section for air transportation in the provisional International Civil Aviation Organisation in Montreal. He prepared the establishment of the Organisation and was appointed to be the main legal adviser and the first director of the ICAO Legal Bureau and the first Secretary of the Legal Committee.[11]

In 1947 he gave a course on air law at the Academy of The Hague.

In 1956 Eugène Pépin published an important work of geography: the geography of air traffic (*Géographie de la navigation aérienne*).[12] As an introduction he displayed a review of the aircraft activity which he followed almost entirely personally. He showed the importance of the two World Wars in the development of aeronautics. In the second part, he envisaged more specifically legal aspects, particularly the problem of the sovereignty of States over the airspace above their territory. In the third part, he treated flows of air traffic and finally he treated the question why this new mode of transport was of interest.

C Activities in the Field of Space Law

I. *The beginning*

At the time of the launch of Sputnik I in 1957, Eugène Pépin was already 70 years old. With a very forward-looking view, he however understood the importance of legal problems created by the development of this new activity. He used his important experience in the creation of air law to see how space law could evolve. While he was directing the Institute of Air Law of the

11 ICAO Report of the work of the Legal Committee 26th Session Montreal, 29 April – 13 May 1987, page 1 at point 2.1., where the Committee paid tribute to Dr. Pépin at the occasion of his forthcoming one-hundredth birthday.

12 Eugène Pépin, Géographie de la Circulation aérienne, 341 et seq. (1956).

University of McGill, the University administration agreed to his application of changing the name of the Institute into "Institute of Air and Space Law".

His inaugural lecture on "Space Law" was given on the 20th April 1959 in front of the students of McGill University. This lecture and many other publications still give evidence of the high intellectual quality of its author.[13] We can see how sharp and critical his view was when he analysed the quality of the doctrine of that time and how accurate his study was of the problems posed by the new activity as well as how efficient he was to propose solutions.

II. Necessity and technique of elaboration of space law

Eugène Pépin supported very early the creation of space law. In the opening lecture of his course on space law at McGill he noted the difficulty of space law being based on practice at a time when so few activities took place. Taking the lessons learned during the creation of air law in which he took such an important part, he supported a voluntary action to establish principles accepted by the States even before the activities took place. He noticed that behaving this way was not usual in the Anglo-Saxon legal culture but insisted on the necessity to do so. As air law had been discussed at the end of the 19th century and at the beginning of the 20th, at a time when aeronautical activities were still very limited, it was necessary to engage in discussions on space law at the very beginning of space activities instead of waiting until States practice would lead to the elaboration of law as usually done within Common Law.

During a lecture given on November 6th, 1957 in front of the Canadian Bar Association,[14] Pépin pointed out that the Chicago Convention which confirmed the States' sovereignty over air space applied only to air space and aircrafts, but not to outer space and spacecrafts.[15] He criticised the partially

13 Eugène Pépin, *Leçon inaugurale du Cours sur le "droit de l'Espace" donnée le 20 avril 1959. See* also: *Introduction to space law* 4 N.Y.L.F. 258 (1958).

14 *Legal problems created by the Sputnik Lecture given on November 6th, 1957 to the Canadian Bar Association in Quebec Maritime and Air Law section, in* 4 McGill.J.(1957-1958), pp. 66 et seq.

15 "Should a launch of a satellite be governed by the rules contained in the Chicago Convention, the answer is clearly: no" ibid., at page 68.

held view to create a three zone system from the Earth to outer space including a continuous zone above 300 or 600 miles above sea level. For him, this was not feasible. Using his knowledge of air law especially of the 1910 discussions during the first conference on sovereignty over air space, he suggested not to discuss this kind of problem but to go directly to practical ones. He insisted on the importance of a lack of protests against the use of outer space for transportation purposes either in the International Committee for the Geophysical Year or by their intention to launch a satellite. For him, the fact that the first satellite was launched by the Soviets and not the Americans was quite useful because, in his opinion, the Soviets were the more likely to refuse the freedom of use of outer space.[16]

III. Freedom of space navigation, liability for space activities

Among the problems which Pépin thought to be expected, he wondered whether satellite circulation should be absolutely free or subject to some kind of regulation, an issue which is still current. In a very pragmatic way, he insisted on the technical aspects of space launches and of the question of the possible fly over of the territory of a foreign State during lift off. He envisaged possible damage when spacecrafts would return to the Earth, the risk of collision in orbit and the need for radio frequencies. He concluded by insisting on the fact that a new convention was needed and that it was not sufficient to amend the Chicago Convention.

IV. Interferences between air navigation and launching of space objects

Given his interest and great qualifications in air law, Pépin was very sensitive to this issue. He considered it as "the most urgent and perhaps the easiest to be resolved".[17]

16 Eugène Pépin indicated that the Soviet Union was not a party to the Chicago Convention but that the rule of soverigny of States over the air above their territoriy was a custom.

17 Eugène Pépin, *Introduction to Space Law*, vol 4 N.Y.L.F. 259 (1958).

V. *Identification and registration of space objects*

When many spacecrafts will be launched it will be necessary to identify the responsible party for damage when ascending or descending to or from the orbit. "Practical measures will be absolutely indispensable".[18]

VI. *Military and peaceful activities*

Pépin remarked the possible utilisation of space objects for military purposes. He noted that the United Nations decided to recognise the necessity to use outer space for peaceful purposes only, but also that the resolution did not make provisions for implementing this rule through a special agreement or through the creation of an organisation. Already in 1959, he suggested the elaboration of a "Declaration" which would solemnly declare that outer space should be used for peaceful purposes only and for the benefit of all countries.

VII. *Limitation of space debris*

Pépin referred to and supported a proposal made in legal literature so as to limit as much as possible the launch of satellites in order to limit the risk of collisions and accidents by limiting the creation of "dead satellites" (*satellites morts*).[19]

VIII. *Proposal of the creation for an International Intergovernmental Organisation*

Remarking that most activities related to outer space would take place outside the national jurisdiction of a state, Pépin suggested the creation of an international or supra-national authority, competent to elaborate the most needed regulation. He had of course in mind an organization like ICAO in the creation of which he had taken such an important part. An international Conference for the creation of such a body should be convened either by

18 Eugène Pépin, *Space penetration*, 52 Am Soc'y Int'l L Proc. 233 et seq. (1958).

19 Eugène Pépin , Les *Problèmes Juridiques de l'espace, Leçon inaugurale du cours sur le droit de l'Espace*, 6 McGill L.J. 41 et seq. (1959-1960).

ICAO or by the UN.[20] He noted that an attempt was made in June 1956 by ICAO.[21] This organisation should work in close cooperation with other specialised agencies like ICAO.[22]

IX. Appropriation of Celestial bodies

Already in 1958 in his "Introduction to Space Law"[23] Eugène Pépin foresaw possible problems which could occur when spacecrafts would land on the Moon. He wondered whether general international law would apply. He indicated that new principles should be adopted.

X. Activities within scientific institutions dealing with space law

Creation of the International Institute of Space Law (IISL)[24]

During the Barcelona International Congress on Astronautics, it was decided to establish a special committee in charge of "defining the respective areas of jurisdiction for air and space law". During the next meeting in 1958, Eugène Pépin proposed an important motion: "The legal problems resulting from the development of astronautics will be solved by a new international convention. Within the framework of the Federation (the International Astronautical Federation) a Permanent Legal Committee should be set up, which should be open to jurists or various associations or groups affiliated with the Federation and whose members would have to study all problems concerning space law to be included in the above mentioned Convention ..." This resolution was adopted by the Ninth Congress of the International

20 Eugène Pépin, *Introduction to Space Law,* 4 New York Law Forum 260 et seq. (1958).

21 Eugène Pépin, *Space penetration,* 52 Am Soc'y Int'l L Proc. 234 et seq. (1958).

22 *See supra,* note 22, at 235.

23 *See supra,* note 21, at 259-261.

24 Eugène Pépin, *The History of the International Institute of Space Law* (1958-1982) on the web site of IISL *available at* http://www.iislweb.org/docs/IISL_History.pdf . See also Stephen Doyle, *The Origins of Space Law and the International Institute of Space Law* on the web site of IISL *available at:*http://www.iislweb.org/docs/Origins_International_Space_Law.pdf.

Astronautical Federation in October 1958. This Permanent Committee was transformed into the International Institute of Space Law in London in 1959. Eugène Pépin became the president of the Institute.

Eugène Pépin was a founding member or member of many institutions working in the field of space law, among them: The International Institute of Space Law IISL (president), the French Society for Air and Space Law, (president in 1984); the French *Académie de l'air et de l'espace* (honorary member); the Space Law Committee of the International Law Association; the International Academy of Astronautics.

D. Conclusion

All these activities just described show that Eugène Pépin was not only a pioneer of air law but also of space law. With his ideas he was instrumental for the development of this new science. All persons who have known him indicate his great intellectual curiosity, his kindness, his physical and moral elegance, his humanism, and his extremely sharp and open mind.

Bibliograpy

The bibliography of Eugène Pépin from 1908 to 1988 takes no less than 21 pages and refers to 276 publications, books and articles mainly on air law and air navigation. One may also find some articles on space law as well as on South America and his native region in France, Touraine, but also on operas and lyric theatre.

Publications relevent in this context are:

Géographie de la circulation aérienne, Paris (Gallimard), 1955, 341pp.

Legal problems created by the Sputnik, 4 McGill Law Journal, 1957-1958, 66-71.

Space Penetration, in 52 Proceedings of the American Society of International Law, 1958. pp. 229-235.

Introduction to Space Law, in: 34 New York Law Forum N. Y. L. F. (1958), pp.258 ff.

Les problèmes juridiques de l'espace, Leçon inaugurale du cours de droit spatial, 6 McGill Law Journal, 1959-1960, pp. 30-42.

Chapter III John Cobb Cooper, Jr. (18.9.1887 – 22.7.1967)

Ram S. Jakhu* and Michelle Ancona**

A. The Man and His Perspective on Space Law

John Cobb Cooper, founder and the first director of the Institute of Air and Space Law at McGill University in Montreal, Canada, was an exceptionally visionary educationalist whose immense intellectual contribution to the development of air and space law makes him undoubtedly the world's leading pioneer in this field. In this short essay, we only highlight a few of his key contributions mainly in the area of space law. In order to provide some background, we start with a brief introduction to Cooper's personal life and his relevant professional activities in the field of air and space law including his own formulation of certain basic concepts relating to sovereignty and flight.

1. *The Man: Lawyer, Naval Officer, Businessman and Diplomat*

Born on September 18, 1887 in Jacksonville, Florida, to Mr. John Cobb and Mrs. Mary Coldwell Cooper,[1] John Cobb Cooper received his elementary education

* Associate Professor, Institute of Air and Space Law, McGill University, Montreal, Canada.

** LL.M. Candidate, Institute of Air and Space Law, McGill University, Montreal, Canada.

1 John Cobb Cooper, Explorations in Aerospace Law, ed. Ivan A. Vlasic, 455 (McGill University Press, 1968).

Stephan Hobe (ed.), Pioneers of Space Law
© 2013 International Institute of Space Law. ISBN *978-90-04-24027-8. pp. 35-47*

in the Jacksonville Public Schools system. He graduated from Lawrenceville School, New Jersey, in 1905 and entered Princeton University that same year. After graduating from Princeton in 1909 with a Bachelor of Arts (A.B.) degree,[2] John Cobb Cooper married Ms. Martha Helen Marvel in 1918 and the couple subsequently had three children.[3]

John Cobb Cooper studied law in the office of Cooper & Cooper in Jacksonville, Florida, and practiced law in the same city between 1911 and 1934 following his admission to the bar through examination by the Supreme Court of Florida in June 1911.[4]

Cooper joined the U.S. Navy during the First World War. Although he was relieved from active service in 1919, he remained a member of the Naval Reserve for several years thereafter and he was promoted to the rank of Lieutenant-Commander.[5]

Cooper's passion for the legal scholarship and the legal profession became evident during his days of legal practice. He founded and became the Editor-in-Chief of the Florida State Bar Association Law Journal during 1927-34,[6] where he became President of the Florida Bar Association in 1931.[7]

Thereafter, Cooper's professional interests and activities became more focused on aviation and particularly aviation law. This started when he was appointed as member of the International Technical Committee of Legal Aerial Experts for 1932-34[8] and, later, in 1933, when President Roosevelt nominated him to serve as the Chairman of the US delegation to the Third

2 William Hildred, C.B., O.B.E. Director General of the International Air Transport Association (1946-66), "Dedication of the Symposium to the Memory of John Cobb Cooper" (August 1967), Session One of the Symposium on the Warsaw Convention, in 33 J. Air L. & Com. 526, 526-527 (1967).

3 Cooper, *supra* note 1.

4 Thea Agape V. Lim, *John Cobb Cooper: At the Frontiers of International Law*, in Canadian Council of International Law, Student Essays in the University of Toronto Project, 2 (Canada 2005-2007).

5 Cooper, *supra* note 1.

6 *Id.*

7 http://www.floridamemory.com/items/show/19976.

8 Cooper, *supra* note 1, at ix and 456.

International Conference on Private Air Law.[9] In that capacity, Cooper had the privilege of signing the Convention on Liability for Damages to Third Parties on the Surface (1933 Rome Convention) as well as the Convention on Precautionary Attachment of Aircraft on behalf of the United States.[10]

Cooper was not only a practicing lawyer and a governmental advisor in aviation legal affairs, but also a businessman in the aviation industry. He was elected and served as Vice President of Pan American World Airways (Pan Am) from 1934 to 1945.[11] During this period, he negotiated route agreements for PanAm's first trans-Atlantic and first trans-Pacific scheduled air services.[12]

Cooper's contribution to the development of aviation law expanded significantly when he served as adviser to the US delegation to, and Chairman of one of the drafting committees of the 1944 Chicago Conference.[13] It is significant to note that this Conference culminated in the adoption of the 1944 Convention on International Civil Aviation (Chicago Convention – the modern constitution for international civil aviation) and also resulted in the establishment of the International Civil Aviation Organization (ICAO) as well as, to a large extent, the eventual formation of the International Air Transport Association (IATA), both located in Montreal, Canada.

At the national level, Cooper was appointed as a consultant to President Truman's Air Policy Commission in 1947,[14] and also served as a consultant to the President's Airport Commission in 1952.[15]

At the international level, Cooper worked as the Legal Advisor at IATA from 1946 to 1964,[16] and participated in the 1948 Geneva Conference which produced the Convention on the International Recognition of Rights in Aircraft; in the 1952 Rome Conference which adopted the Convention on Damage Caused by Foreign Aircraft to Third Parties on the Surface (1952

9 Cooper, *supra* note 1, at 456.

10 Cooper, *supra* note 1, at ix.

11 Cooper, *supra* note 1, at x and 456.

12 Cooper, *supra* note 1, at x.

13 Cooper, *supra* note 9.

14 *Id.*

15 Cooper, *supra* note 1, at 457.

16 Cooper, *supra* note 1, at 456 – 457.

Rome Convention); and, in the 1955 Hague Conference that produced the Hague Protocol of 1955.

During a period of five years (1946-1951), Cooper was elected as a member of the Institute for Advanced Study in Princeton where he conducted research in international air law under a grant from the Rockefeller Foundation.[17] It was during this period that Cooper published his seminal book titled *The Right to Fly* (1947). This book is considered to be "a masterful analysis of the many independent factors – historical, political, economic, military and geographic – which determined the aviation policies of nation-states and, ultimately, the international law of the air."[18]

Cooper's passion for legal scholarship and legal education was rekindled in a desire to disseminate the unique aviation law expertise he had acquired during the course of his career. This led him to establish in 1951 the Institute of International Air Law, later renamed the Institute of Air and Space Law at McGill University in Montreal. Cooper obtained an LL.M. degree from McGill University in 1952.[19] He was appointed the first director of, and a Professor of International Air Law at the Institute from 1951 to 1958, after which he was befittingly designated Professor Emeritus.[20]

On account of Cooper's unique academic and scholarly achievements in the field of air and space law an honorary Doctor of Laws (LL.D.) degree was conferred upon him in 1960 by his *alma mater*, Princeton University.[21] He was also the recipient of the very first Gold Medal awarded by the International Institute of Space Law (IISL) in 1961. Not surprisingly, he was elected as President of the IISL for 1961-1962.[22]

17 Lim, *supra* note 4, at 5.

18 Cooper, *supra* note 1, at x and 456.

19 John Cobb Cooper, *The Manned Orbiting Laboratory: A Major Legal and Political Decision*, 51 A.B.A. J. 1137, 1137-1140 (1965) at 1139.

20 Cooper, *supra* note 15.

21 http://www.princeton.edu/main/about/facts/honorary (Last visited July 16, 2012).

22 Cooper, *supra* note 15.

2. *"Aerospace Law": The Birth of an Idea*

In recent years, several successes have been achieved in the development of technology that enables humans to travel through air space to the edge of outer space at the very least. The use of sub-orbital and, in the not too distant future, orbital space flights for point-to-point travel on the surface of the earth via outer space is becoming commonplace. These advances have given rise to the need for a uniform global legal regime to govern transport activities that take place in the air space and in outer space with various kinds of 'flying' machines, and it has been advocated that this uniform regime should be known as aerospace law.[23]

As far back as 1951, Cooper had postulated that "the scope of Air Law will thus be seen to include man-made and man-controlled movement of any flight instrumentality in all space above and beyond the surface of the earth."[24] The basis of his thesis was that "... Air Law... requires a new accurate determination as to the three fundamental elements involved: (1) the nature and extent of the areas in space where 'Air Law' is applicable; (2) the forms of human activity to be regulated in those areas; and (3) the instrumentalities involved."[25] He also warned that "[i]f this broad view of the scope of Air Law be not accepted, arbitrary and illogical distinctions must be made between various types of flight instrumentalities with resulting practical and legal confusion."[26] Later, in 1963, Cooper correctly anticipated future technological developments when he professed that as "the terms *Air Law* and *Space Law* are now used, they represent nothing more than phases of the law directly and indirectly applicable to man-made flight. To avoid existing and future

23 Ram S. Jakhu, Tommaso Sgobba and Paul Stephen Dempsey (eds.), The Need for an Integrated Regulatory Regime for Aviation and Space: ICAO for Space? (Vienna; New York: Springer, 2011).

24 John Cobb Cooper, *Air Law – A Field for International Thinking* (1951), in Explorations in Aerospace Law 13 (Ivan A. Vlasic ed., McGill University Press, 1968).

25 *Id.* at 4.

26 Cooper, *supra* note 24.

confusion, both should be included in a single branch of the law. This might be termed *Aerospace Law*."[27]

3. *Sovereignty over the Air Space and Freedom in Outer Space*

In many of his writings, Cooper explained: (i) the old 'legal concept of States' territorial rights' and its evolution, as well as the historical assumption of the rights of States to regulate activities occurring in the airspace over their land and waters; (ii) the similarities between the terms 'air' and 'airspace' and the use of these terms in other languages and conventions; and (iii) the constitution of the atmospheric layers with scientific facts to illustrate the speed and altitude that can be achieved with then available technology.

According to Cooper, the "territory of a State, geographically considered, is a three dimensional region. It includes an area on the surface of the earth, a sector of the earth below, and a sector of space above. Legally considered, the territory of the State may be defined as those regions in which the State is recognized by international law as having the right to exercise national sovereignty to the exclusion of all other States."[28] It was Cooper's opinion that "... The territory of the State extends upward *at least* as far above the surface as to include a region which can be roughly defined as 'airspace'."[29] Consequently, since "international law contains no presently [i.e. in 1951] accepted rule covering the question as to whether usable space above and beyond the 'airspace' is or is not part of the territory of the State below."[30] Cooper asserted that outer space is free for exploration and use by all States. Cooper proclaimed that "we must abandon the theory that the State has the right to claim territory in outer space as far as the earth's attraction extends, and that we must admit some such reasonable rules [...] namely, that at any particular time the territory of each State extends upward into space as far

27 John Cobb Cooper, *Aerospace Law – Subject Matter and Terminology*, 29 J.Air L. & Com., 89, 89-96 (1963) at 89.

28 John Cobb Cooper, *High Altitude Flight and National Sovereignty* (1951), in Explorations in Aerospace Law 257 (Ivan A. Vlasic ed., McGill University Press, 1968).

29 *Id.* at 260.

30 *Id.*

as then (SIC) scientific progress of any State in the international community permits such State to control space above it."[31]

It is interesting to note that in 1951 when Cooper put forth his assertion of freedom of outer space, he believed that this was his own original idea. He later realized that previously, others had expressed similar views. Cooper eloquently admitted that:

> It was the author's misfortune that he had not heard of the German language pamphlet by Vladimir Mandl, published in 1932, entitled Das Weltraumrecht: ein Problem der Raumfahrt, *i.e.*, The Law of Outer space, a Problem of Space Flight. In 1951, this author said, In the first place [...] we must agree that there is an upper boundary in space to the territory of the subjacent State. In 1932, as I found long after, Mandl had said, speaking of air sovereignty: But this sovereignty must have a territorial boundary somewhere and it cannot extend endlessly. This question is, at what distance from the ground this boundary should be set. Had Mandl's work been known to the author during his years of research at the Institute for Advanced Study in Princeton, he would have discussed it in this paper and given due credit to the thinking of the real pioneer, but no reference to Mandl's essay had appeared in English.[32]

Cooper's postulation of the fundamental legal principle of freedom in outer space was based on several historical, legal, and technical and scientific considerations. As far back as 1958, Cooper had determined that:

(1) Rockets, high altitude guided missiles, satellites and future spaceships are not aircrafts and their flight is not governed by any existing agreement or regulation.
(2) States have sovereignty in their airspace above their surface territories and the right to control flight therein. This airspace includes only areas where sufficient gaseous atmosphere exists to provide aerodynamic lift for such flight instrumentalities as balloons and aircrafts.

31 *Id.* at 264.
32 Cooper, *supra* note 28.

(3) Rockets, guided missiles and satellites are actually being used today in areas of 'outer space' beyond the territorial sphere of any State, entirely unregulated, and beyond the rule of law.

(4) No agreement exists as to where the boundary is between the territorial airspace of a State and outer space beyond – nor as to the legal status of the intermediate area lying between the territorial airspace and outer space, in which intermediate area the presence of a certain amount of gaseous atmosphere may cause the fall of flight instrumentalities, thus endangering the State below.[33]

Cooper understood the challenges of trying to establish an international legal framework for outer space based on predetermined altitudes in air space, mainly because of the constantly evolving technology. Therefore, he cautioned "it would be unfortunate if the international rules of the future high altitude flight control were adopted, and if it were then found that they were based on incorrect theories as to the physical characteristics and usefulness of various areas in the upper atmosphere and beyond."[34] For him, the "only practical way to solve the question as to the legal status of areas above those covered by a strict construction of Article I of the Chicago Convention will be the adoption of some form of international agreement."[35] The international community seems to have followed Cooper's suggestion as the UN General Assembly in its first resolution on outer space in 1958 recognized "the common interest of mankind in outer space" and resolved that outer space "should be used for peaceful purposes only… [b]earing in mind the provision of Article 2, paragraph 1, of the Charter of the United Nations, which States that the Organization is based on the principle of the sovereign equality of all its Members."[36] This view has firmly been incorporated into Article I of

33 John Cobb Cooper, *Missiles and Satellites: The Law and Our National Policy* 44 A.B.A. J. 317, 317-321 (1958) at 321.

34 John Cobb Cooper, *Legal Problems of Upper Space* (1956), in EXPLORATIONS IN AEROSPACE LAW 276 (Ivan A. Vlasic ed., McGill University Press, 1968).

35 *Id.* at 275.

36 UN General Assembly Resolution 1348 (XIII) of 13 December 1958.

the 1967 Outer Space Treaty,[37] to which there are over 100 States Parties at present.

4. *Boundary between Air Space and Outer Space*[38]

If there is national sovereignty over a State's air space and outer space is free for exploration and use by all States, it is logical that there ought to be a demarcation between national air space and international outer space. Almost all pioneers of space law as well as the international community have addressed the issue of the boundary between air space and outer space. It was one of the first space law-related items to be considered by the United Nations in 1959.[39] Since then, the issue has remained unresolved.[40] It is interesting to see Cooper's standpoint on one of the most fundamental and controversial legal questions of space law that relates to the determination of the application or otherwise of the law governing outer space.

Cooper was always concerned with the emergence of a new area of law given that science and technology were evolving very rapidly thereby resulting in an ever-widening gap between the state of technology and the state of the law. He pointed out the need to define a geographical area where the international legal principles were to apply so as to achieve legal certainty forevery State within the international community regarding the limits of national sovereignty. In his writings, he would usually include a detailed explanation of the factual and scientific information known and available to him dealing with atmospheric heights, density, temperatures and impact on balloons, aircrafts and rockets. In some cases, he would venture to suggest a

37 *Treaty on Principles Governing the Activities of States in the Exploration and Use of Outer Space, Including the Moon and Other Celestial Bodies*, Jan. 27, 1967, 610 U.N.S.T. 205 (entered into force Oct. 10, 1967).

38 Cooper, *supra* note 28, at 263 and *supra* note 34, at 275.

39 *Question of Determining Where Outer Space Begins*, Report of the Legal Committee, Ad Hoc Committee on the Peaceful Usesof Outer Space, UN Document A/AC.98/2 of June 12, 1959, at 7.

40 *Report of the Legal Subcommittee on its fifty-first session*, held in Vienna from 19 to 30 March 2012, United Nations Committee on the Peaceful Uses of Outer Space, UN Document A/AC.105/1003 of April 10, 2012, at 12.

determined altitude limit to separate outer space and the space where States had the legal right to control their airspace.

In the end, what he was mainly concerned about was the establishment of a definition of outer space and its boundaries with respect to airspace.

According to Cooper, "we must agree that there is an upper boundary in space to the territory of the subjacent State" and "the outer boundary of the State cannot be further than the point where the earth's attraction will govern the movement of an object in space so that such object will 'fall' onto the earth. On the other hand, this boundary cannot be lower than the upper limit of airspace. ... [Therefore] it would appear that the upper boundary of the State's territory lies at a point between the upper limit of the 'airspace' and the upper limit of the earth's attraction."[41]

In 1958, Cooper expressed the view that "[T]he regulations adopted by the International Civil Aviation Organization for the control of international flight apply to aircraft and to aircraft only. These are defined as including "all machines which can derive support in the atmosphere from reactions of the air". Satellites and rockets do not depend for their support upon the presence of gaseous air."[42]

Cooper felt that United Nations should determine the line of demarcation between airspace and outer space. As a jurist, he was of the opinion that "outer space law must determine and state the rights of States to use the area which we call 'outer space,' and must, at the same time, fix the area in which such international rights exist."[43] For the purpose of such demarcation, Cooper felt the need for an international agreement. Thus, in 1960, Cooper suggested that "in an international convention dealing with flight into outer space, the following statement might be included: 'Outer space, for the purposes of this convention, is defined as the area above earth's surface at which

41 Cooper, *supra* note 34, at 275.

42 Cooper, *supra* note 33, at 318.

43 John Cobb Cooper, *Current Developments in Space Law* at Southeastern Regional Meeting of the American Society of International Law (1963) in 41 N.C. L. Rev. 339, 339-353, (1962-1963), at 347.

an artificial satellite may be put in orbit at least once around the earth, and whose upper or outer boundary is the outer limit of our solar system'."[44]

5. *The Law of the Sea as a basis for the Law of Outer Space*

As the principle of 'freedom to fly over the high seas' by aircraft belonging to both coastal and noncoastal States became a feature of the law of sea conventions, Cooper acknowledged that "[s]lowly and inexorably we are coming to accept the fact that the legal status of outer space and the high seas differs very little, if at all."[45] To him, it was "necessary to assign the same status to outer space areas above the high seas and above national lands and waters of sovereign states. It would be quite impossible to consider a situation in which a spacecraft [...] found itself theoretically subject to one rule over the high seas and a different one over a subjacent state."[46] Cooper's belief in using law of the sea as a basis for the law of outer space also influenced his thoughts on the nationality and registration of spacecraft.

6. *Nationality and Registration of Spacecraft*

As early as 1961, Cooper recognized the necessity to determine the nationality of each spacecraft for purposes of ascribing State responsibility for national implementation of a State's international obligations accepted under international agreements governing space activities. According to him, every "flight instrumentality usable in outer space must have the nationality of a state of the international community. Normally, this would be the launching state, which will thereby become responsible for the behavior of the satellite, or other spacecraft so far as rules of international law are concerned."[47]

44 John Cobb Cooper, *Fundamental Questions of Outer Space Law* lecture Presented at Leiden University (10 October 10, 1960) in Explorations in Aerospace Law (Ivan A. Vlasic ed., McGill University Press, 1968), at 291.

45 John Cobb Cooper, *The Manned Orbiting Laboratory: A Major Legal and Political Decision* (1965), in Explorations in Aerospace Law, 429 (Ivan A. Vlasic ed., McGill University Press, 1968).

46 *Id.* at 430.

47 John Cobb Cooper, *The Rule of Law in Outer Space* 47 A.B.A. J. 23, 23-27 (1961), at 26.

Cooper's idea of nationality of space flight instrumentalities was derived from the law of the sea and also from the provisions of the 1944 the Chicago Convention that require aircraft to bear the nationality and registration marks of their State of registry. Thus according to Cooper, "... a state gives to a ship the right to use its flag, such state assumes certain international responsibilities for the good conduct of that ship on the high seas and in the foreign ports and at the same time acts as the protector of the ship to enforce its international rights. [...] While the application of the rule of nationality to rockets and satellites may be difficult, nevertheless if upper space is to be free like the high seas, then certainly a state must be prepared to be responsible for the international good conduct of its rockets and satellites; otherwise chaos will result."[48]

Cooper perceived the possibility of joint operation of satellites by several States as well as by international organizations and consequently recognized the need for an international register of spacecraft. He felt the necessity, "for practical purposes that all spacecraft, whether civil or state, should be uniformly registered, and that provision be made by international convention that no object be launched into space unless or until the provision of national and international registration have been carried out."[49] As we know, the provisions of Articles VI and VIII of the 1967 Outer Space Treaty and the 1975 Registration Convention[50] contain principles similar to those suggested by Cooper.

B. Conclusion

Cooper was indeed a pioneer in space law as he was actively involved in most, if not all, of the history surrounding the evolution and politics of air law and space law.

48 Cooper *supra* note 34, at 277.

49 John Cobb Cooper, *A study on the Legal Status of the Aircraft (1949)*, author supplemental note *Basic Problems of Spacecraft Nationality* (1966), in Explorations in Aerospace Law (Ivan A. Vlasic ed., McGill University Press, 1968) at 254.

50 *Convention on Registration of Objects Launched into Outer Space*, adopted by the UN General Assembly under Resolution 3235 (XXIX) of 12 November 1974, entered into force on 15 September 1976, 1023 U.N.T.S. 15.

He was one of a few scholarly publicists of space law who fully understood the interdisciplinary nature of this field of law that closely intertwined legal issues in global historical and political events and the technical and scientific developments related to outer space. Based on this knowledge, he laid a solid foundation for the formulation of basic principles of space law and suggested the way forward to unify air law and space law into aerospace law. Recent technological developments that enable 'aerospacecraft' to travel seamlessly in airspace and outer space clearly show that Cooper was a visionary, far ahead of his time.

Chapter IV **Evgeny Aleksandrovich Korovin** (12.10.1892 – 3.11.1964)

Gennady P. Zhukov,* Vladlen S. Vereshchetin** and Anatoly Y. Kapustin***

In 2012, the legal community commemorated the 120th anniversary of the birth of one of the pioneers of space law, a Corresponding Member of the USSR Academy of Sciences, Honored Scientist of the Russian Federation, Doctor of Law, Professor Evgeny Aleksandrovich Korovin.

The history of the Russian science of international law is inextricably linked with the name of E.A. Korovin. He was a prominent international lawyer, scholar, diplomat and public figure.

E.A. Korovin is also considered the founder of the Russian science of space law, in whose origin he played a singular role.

As far back as in 1933, at a meeting of specialists on air law in Leningrad, E.A. Korovin delivered a lecture on the new legal problems arising in connection with the prospects of human flights in higher layers of air space (stratosphere). One year later, his article on the same subject was published in the French journal "Revue Générale de Droit International Public".[1] Even though the author did not specifically deal in this article with the legal regime of

* Professor of International Law of the Russian University of Peoples' Friendship.

** Professor of International Law.

*** Professor of International Law, President of the Russian Association of International Law.

1 Eugène Korovine, *La conquête de la stratosphère et le droit international,* XLI Revue Générale de Droit International Public, 675-686 (1934).

Stephan Hobe (ed.), Pioneers of Space Law
© *2013 International Institute of Space Law.* ISBN *978-90-04-24027-8. pp. 49-55*

space beyond the atmosphere, his concluding remarks are now fully applicable to the activities in outer space. He wrote: "The international cooperation of all States inspired by the desire to guarantee peace, regional and global security, and resolved to stop by all means any attempts of aggression, appears to be the only way to ensure peaceful exploration of stratosphere in the framework of existing international law".[2]

In 1958, the work of E.A. Korovin was estimated by the Hugo Grotius International Foundation in Germany as "a great contribution to the creation of international space law" and he was awarded the Hugo Grotius Medal.

In 1959, E.A. Korovin published an article on the international status of outer space in the Soviet journal "International Affairs". This was the first attempt in the Soviet literature to deal comprehensively with some core issues of space law. Under his editorship two collections of articles on space law problems were published in the Soviet Union in 1962: one included the articles written by Soviet authors, the other – the translation of essays written by foreign jurists.

In 1959, at the initiative of E.A. Korovin, the USSR Academy of Sciences established the Commission on Legal Questions of Interplanetary Space which consisted of the researchers from the Institute of State and Law (E.G. Vasilevkaya, G.P. Zhukov, G.P. Zadorozhny, P.I. Lukin), from the Ministry of Foreign Affairs (F.N. Kovalev, G.A. Osnitskaya, I.I. Cheprov) and from the Staff of the Presidium of the Academy of Sciences – V.S. Vereshchetin. E.A. Korovin was appointed Chairman. The Commission also included a number of very competent technical experts. In its work, it relied on the valuable advice of these experts and enjoyed the support of several well-known members of the Academy (academicians): A.A. Blagonravov, B.N. Petrov, E.K. Fedorov and L.I. Sedov.

The Commission regularly sent its views and recommendations on the legal aspects of space exploration to the Presidium of the Academy of Sciences and to the Ministry of Foreign Affairs of the USSR. Chairman of the Commission E.A. Korovin was directly involved in research on space law topics and was constantly occupied with the current work of the Commission. It is noteworthy that at a time when there was a great need for the elaboration of basic principles governing States in their space activities E.A. Korovin

2 *Id.* at 685-686.

gathered around him a team of lawyers, diplomats and technical experts who contributed to the formation of nascent rules of international space law, in particular those relating to the Declaration of Legal Principles.

Thus, the Commission participated in the detailed legal substantiation of the position of Soviet delegations at the COPUOS Legal Sub-Committee sessions in 1962 and 1963 held in New York.[3] The Secretary of the Commission G.P. Zhukov was a member of the Soviet delegations to these sessions. E.A. Korovin and the Commission which he chaired endeavoured to maintain a close link between legal theory and practical astronautics as well as between space lawyers and technical experts in the field of space activities.

In 1961, the Institute of State and Law created a special Working Group of the Commission to study topical space law issues. The Group was composed of three lawyers: E.G. Vasilevskaya, G.P. Zhukov (Head of the Group) and P.I. Lukin. Once a month, a plenary meeting of the Commission was convened to discuss important issues of international space law. Among the issues dealt with by the Commission one might mention the legal basis for proposing a treaty boundary between air and outer space at an altitude of 100-110 km above the sea level. Later it was used in preparing the official proposals of the Soviet delegations in 1979 and 1983. The Commission also participated in the process of drafting the Soviet proposals concerning basic principles of the activities of States in the exploration and peaceful uses of outer space, which were presented by the USSR on September 10, 1962 and on April 16, 1963 in the COPUOS Legal Subcommittee.

Using his vast knowledge and experience, E.A. Korovin combined his fruitful scientific work with training young generations of lawyers and carrying out multifaceted public activities. As has already been mentioned, two collections of articles on space law were prepared under his guidance or editorship. On one of them ("Space and International Law"[4]) the world's first cosmonaut Yuri Gagarin made the following inscription: "To theorists with the wish to work out the most just legal rules in outer space. Practitioner Yuri Gagarin. 12/07/62."

3 UN.Doc.A / AC. 105C.2/L.2, UN.Doc.A/AC.105C.2/L.6.

4 E.A. Korovin, Space and International Law, M. IMO, (1962).

At the initiative of Korovin, in 1962, a group of Soviet lawyers, with his participation, attended the International Colloquium on Space Law organized in the framework of the International Astronautical Congress in Varna.

E.A. Korovin presented there a report on Urgent Tasks of Space Law. He also promoted a more active participation of Soviet space lawyers in the work of the International Institute of Space Law. In his writings and lectures E.A. Korovin emphasized that no State had a right to threaten the security of another State or cause damage to its citizens or property. This elementary rule of modern international law should be applied equally on land and at sea, in air and in outer space.

Unfortunately, soon after the death of E.A. Korovin in 1964, the Commission of the Academy of Sciences on Legal Questions of Interplanetary Space practically ceased to function. Formally, it finished its work in October 1973 when the Presidium of the USSR Academy of Sciences received a letter from Deputy Foreign Minister S.P. Kozyrev – Head of a newly created organ under the auspices of the Ministry of Foreign Affairs.[5] The letter stated that in view of the establishment of the Interdepartmental Commission on Political and Legal Questions Relating to the Exploration and Uses of Outer Space, the Foreign Ministry considered inadvisable the existence of a parallel body in the Academy of Sciences.

At the same time, by a decision of the Academy, the coordination of scientific research in the field of space law remained the responsibility of the academic Institute of State and Law.[6]

Korovin belonged to the galaxy of eminent pre-revolutionary Russian lawyers: Sergey B. Krylov, Vsevolod N. Durdenevsky, Ivan S. Peretersky and Viktor E. Grabar. After the revolution, they all made an enormous contribution to the teaching of students and the development of the Soviet doctrine of international law.

At the beginning of the 1920s at Moscow State University there was established a Department of International Relations with a view to train a new generation of diplomats. E.A. Korovin taught them international law. After

5 Oleg Khlestov, *Cosmos-the future of humanity*, Russian News, April 11, 2007.

6 The Academy of Sciences appointed Vice-President and Legal Counsel of INTERCOSMOS V.S. Vereshchetin as its representative in the newly established interdepartmental Commission.

the Second World War, for many years he held the Chair and lectured international law at the Higher Diplomatic School of the Soviet Foreign Ministry.

E.A. Korovin not only took part in training diplomats, but he himself was actively involved in diplomatic work as a member of the Board of the Ministry of Foreign Affairs and as a participant of many international diplomatic meetings and conferences.

From 1918 to 1927, E.A. Korovin was Secretary of the Central Committee of the Russian Red Cross Society and head of its foreign department. In 1929 and 1945, he was a Soviet Union expert at the Conference on Air Law in Paris. In 1945 – he was an expert of the delegation of the USSR in the Preparatory Commission for the United Nations Organization; in 1945-1946 – he was an expert at the London and Paris sessions of the Council of Foreign Ministers. In 1956-1961, he represented the USSR in various UNESCO Committees.

E.A. Korovin was a member of the Permanent Court of Arbitration and a member of the Maritime Arbitration Commission of the USSR, President of the legal section of the All-Union Society for Cultural Relations with Foreign Countries.

In 1935, he was elected as a member of the Academy of Political Science (New York), gave lectures at the University of Paris and at The Hague Academy of International Law. In 1936, he became a member of the American Society of International Law. In 1946, E.A. Korovin was elected as a corresponding member of the USSR Academy of Sciences.

E.A. Korovin authored 11 books and over 150 pamphlets and articles published in Russian, Ukrainian, Belarusian, English, French, German and Japanese on various issues of international politics and international law. He is the author of the first Soviet international law courses: "International Law in Transition Time" (1924) and "Modern Public International Law" (1926). The titles of his books and studies vividly demonstrate the range of his scientific interests: "Catholicism as a Factor in Contemporary World Politics" (1931), "The USSR and Disarmament" (1933, in English), "Japan and International Law" (1936), "The Laws of War" (1944), "History of International Law" (1946), Studies on the French Revolution of 1789 and International Organization of Peace and Security (1945-46), "The Main Problems of Contemporary International Relations" (1959), "International Law: a textbook for use in law schools" (1961, in English). E.A. Korovin also co-authored two textbooks on international law, published in 1951 and 1957.

In his scholarly writings, lectures and reports E.A. Korovin analyzed such topical theoretical problems of the time as the notion of modern international law, the concept of sovereignty in international law, national self-determination, the development of the principle of peaceful coexistence and many others.

E.A. Korovin actively participated in the social, cultural and political life of the country. He was a member of the editorial boards of the Soviet journal "International Affairs", and the "Soviet Yearbook of International Law." He was also involved in the activities of such organizations as the Soviet United Nations Association, the Society for Dissemination of Political and Scientific Knowledge, the Society of Friendship between the USSR and France. For his distinguished scholarly teaching and diplomatic activities E.A. Korovin was awarded several high national orders of the Soviet Union: "Order of Lenin", "Order of Labour Red Banner", "Order of the Badge of Honour" and many State's medals.

From 1947 to 1952, E.A. Korovin worked as Director of the Academy of Sciences Institute of Law[7] – the principal research organization of the country in the field of law. This was the time of the last years of Stalin's repressions. One villainous campaign was followed by another. In that period, one of the authors of the present article (G.P. Zhukov) was a postgraduate student at the Institute of Law, and E.A. Korovin was his scientific supervisor. He confirms first-hand that in those years which were difficult for the country the behaviour of Professor E.A. Korovin was beyond reproach. He never participated either in the "anti-cosmopolitan" or any other campaigns against imaginary "enemies of the Soviet people". The fact that E.A. Korovin was not a member of the Communist Party evidently helped him to avoid any involvement in those campaigns despite his high official position in the Academy of Sciences.

We would like to finish this tribute to the memory of E.A. Korovin by mentioning an interesting detail of his biography which remained unknown until recently. Specialists in the study of literature had known absolutely nothing about the author of the book "My Alcove: poems" published in Moscow in 1916. Until recently, unexpectedly, it was found that the world-renowned jurist, one of the founders of space law, Professor E.A. Korovin and the author

7 Later it was renamed as Institute of State and Law.

of this book were one and the same person. His brilliant poetic debut, including an excellent translation of French poetry, coincided with his graduation in 1915 from the law faculty of Moscow University when he was twenty-three years old.

Chapter V **Vladimír Mandl** (20.3.1899 – 8.1.1941)

Vladimír Kopal* and Mahulena Hofmann**

A. Introduction

In a keynote address on "A Concise History of Space Law" by Stephen E. Doyle (USA), which was delivered during the 53rd Colloquium of the International Institute of Space Law (IISL) at the 61st International Astronautical Congress held in Prague, 2010, the speaker also mentioned a Czech lawyer, Professor Vladimír Mandl, as author of the world's first comprehensive survey of space law.[1] After that address, V. Kopal made an intervention on the life and work of Vladimír Mandl.[2] Stephan Hobe dedicated a substantive attention to Mandl's work in his paper at the same session.[3]

Already in 1968, V. Kopal presented a report on the life and work of Vladimír Mandl at the Second History Symposium of the International Academy of Astronautics (IAA), which was held in conjunction with the XIX

* Professor of International Law, Faculty of Law, West Bohemian University, Plzeň (Pilsen), Czech Republic. Former Chief of the UN Outer Space Affairs Division in New York and later on Chairman of the Legal Subcommittee, United Nations Committee on the Peaceful Uses of Outer Space (COPUOS).

** Professor of Law, SES Chair in Satellite Communications and Media Law, Faculty of Law, Economics and Finance in the University of Luxembourg, Luxembourg.

1 Proceedings of the International Institute of Space Law, 2010. Published and distributed by the American Institute of Aeronautics and Astronautics, 2011, p. 4.

2 *Id.* at 18 *et seq.*

3 *Id.* at 21 *et seq.*

Stephan Hobe (ed.), Pioneers of Space Law
© 2013 *International Institute of Space Law.* ISBN *978-90-04-24027-8. pp. 57-69*

International Astronautical Congress in New York.[4] He then occasionally referred to Mandl's fundamental role in the evolution of the doctrine of space law in some other papers and lectures.[5]

The contribution to this book is a revised and completed version of these papers, based on further research and offering a wider image of the life and work of Professor Vladimír Mandl.

B. Mandl's Studies, Early Publications and Doctorate

Vladimír Mandl was born on March 20, 1899 as son of Dr. Matouš Mandl, an estimable attorney-at-law in Plzeň (Pilsen), an industrial city, which was at that time a part of the Austrian-Hungarian Empire. After the defeat and split of that monarchy in World War I, Pilsen became one of the major cities of the newly born Czechoslovakia, now located in the present Czech Republic.

Following his studies at the Pilsener high school, Vladimír Mandl entered the Czech Faculty of Law, Charles University of Prague, where he studied for eight semesters. In particular, he became a member of the seminar on civil law procedure, which was guided by an outstanding scholar, Professor Václav Hora. After his graduation to Doctor of Law on November 24, 1921, Mandl shortly practiced at a district court in Prague and then for some time in his father's office, but on March 1, 1927, having successfully passed the advocate examinations, he opened his own office of attorney-at-law in Pilsen. Thus, though he was originally thinking of engineering studies and profession, he decided to follow his father's legal career.

Mandl's original civil law orientation led him to write first papers in that legal field. In 1925 Mandl contributed to the first Congress of the Czechoslovak Lawyers by a report on problems of evidence and in 1926 he completed a monograph on the Czechoslovak civil law relating to marriage.

4 Vladimír Kopal, *Vladimír Mandl: Founding Writer on Space*, which was published in: First Steps toward Space, edited by Frederic C. Durant III and George S. James, Smithsonian Institution Press, City of Washington, 1974, p. 87 *et seq.*

5 *See* e.g. *Evolution of the Doctrine of Space Law*, in: Space Law, Development and Scope, edited by N. Jasentualiyana, Praeger, Westport, Connecticut, London, 1992, p. 17 *et seq.*, especially pp. 18-19.

Nevertheless, Mandl's original technical vocation turned his interest soon to legal problems created by industrial and technological developments of the 1920s and 1930s. At first, he published a series of articles, and later on in 1929 a monograph, on legal aspects of motor vehicles.[6] But it was quite natural that his attention was also drawn to legal problems of aviation. His studies in the new discipline resulted in a monograph on air law, which was published by the Pilsener Aeroclub in 1928.[7] That work was in fact the first treatise on this topic written in the Czech language. After a historical introduction, the author dealt with the Czechoslovak air regulation accomplished by the Law on Civil Aviation in 1925. In the second part, he considered some special problems of air law, such as liability arising from international air transport contracts, conflicts of law concerning aviation, customs and insurance against damage caused by aircraft. The final chapter dealt with aerial warfare.

Another outcome of Mandl's law studies was printed in Germany, under the title "Das Tschechoslowakische Luftverkehrgesetz" (Czechoslovak Law of Aviation) and a study on the 1919 Paris Convention in Czech.[8] Later on, Mandl also started to publish some of his air law studies in other countries.[9] And his literary involvement in the field of aviation and air law was followed by a practical step: Following the examples of some early air law pioneers, who acquired balloon or pilot licenses, Mandl also obtained his pilot license in 1929.

C. Mandl's Postgraduate Studies and Habilitation

Dr. Vladimír Mandl submitted his monographical study on air law to the Czech Technical University in Prague, one of the oldest institutions of this kind in Central Europe, as a habilitation thesis in order to become a docent at its Faculty of Mechanical and Electrical Engineering. Documents

6 Vladimír Mandl, Automobilový Zákon z 9. Srpna 1908 A Jeho Reforma (The Automobile Act of August 9, 1908 and its Reform), Praha 1929.

7 Vladimír Mandl, Letecké Právo (Air Law), Plzeň, 1928.

8 Vladimír Mandl, Mezinárodní Úmluva O Úpravě Letectví Ze Dne 13. Října 1910 (International Convention on the Regulation of Aviation of October 13, 1919), Praha, 1932.

9 E.g. Vladimír Mandl, *Le Parachute*, in: La révue générale de droit aérien, Paris, Nos 2, 3, 4/1935.

deposited in the Archives of the Universities of Prague give evidence that Mandl fulfilled all requirements and his knowledge and scholarly work were highly evaluated. Therefore, he received the unanimous approval of the Accreditation Commission. On April 30, 1930, he also delivered a usual test lecture before the Board of Professors of the Faculty on "Liability of Contractors for Damage", a subject that was important at that time due to the conclusion of the 1929 Warsaw Convention on Unification of Certain Rules for the Liability of International Air Transport Operators. The Board of Professors of the Faculty decided by a great majority to grant him a *venia docendi* ("Private docent" in Central European terminology) for the subject matter "Law of Industrial Enterprises" and this decision was then confirmed by the Czechoslovak Minister of Education on September 30, 1932.[10]

In the meantime, Vladimír Mandl also passed his postgraduate studies at the Faculty of Law of the Friedrich Alexander University of Erlangen in Germany and there he successfully defended a thesis on the civil law structure of the right of indemnification. In this way, he continued and extended his original background in civil law. Mandl's work was approved by the Faculty on June 20, 1931 and its author was granted the doctorate of the Erlangen University. His thesis was printed in Germany the same year.[11]

Mandl's work dealt with the absolute liability in civil law and may be assessed today also in the light of the subsequent UN Convention on International Liability for Damage Caused by Space Objects of 1972. The first chapter of Mandl's thesis was devoted to the basis of civil right relations – the expression of will. The chapter with a title "The Will to Damage" ("Der Schadenswillen") concentrated on the liability without fault. The basis of this form of liability is a violation of "protective" legal norms aimed at the most dangerous human activities such as operating of industrial facilities or driving transport vehicles.

As in his further works, Mandl approached legal problems from the point of morality. He thought that in comparison with other individuals, the disposal of those dangerous objects puts their owners in a special, preferential position. This specific advantage has to be compensated by a strict form

10 Decree of the Minister of Education No. 892 12/31-IV/3 of September 30, 1932.

11 Vladimír Mandl, Zivilistischer Aufbau des Schadenersatzrechtes, Verlag von M. and H. Marcus, Breslau, 1932. This study includes Mandl's own *curriculum vitae.*

of protection of the public, which is not connected with the motives of fault of the owner but is based solely on the fact of violation of legal norms: "Each invocation of legal remedy... based on the extraordinary burden for the general public results in a liability title of the damaged."[12] Mandl underlined this conclusion by drawing a comparison to the liability based on penal law and concluded that civil law did not recognize any good or bad will, but only one will. The ideal, ethical aspects of the behavior of the subject of dangerous activities must not lead to any material or economic disadvantage of the damaged, but solely to their full compensation.

D. Mandl's Orientation to Astronautics and Space Law

By that time, Mandl also started to attach a growing importance to a new possible field of human endeavors – the rise and development of activities in outer space. Influenced by the publications of the contemporary thinkers about and experimentalists with rockets as means for access to space, Mandl accomplished two works.

The first one was a booklet on the problem of interstellar transport, which was published in order to address a wider circle of readers in his own country.[13] His booklet opened with a brief survey of developments in astronautics, in which he described the work of Konstantin Tsiolkovski, Robert H. Goddard, Franz von Hoefft, Hermann Oberth and others. In the second part, he explained the basic principles of rocketry. The publication also included Mandl's own design of a high altitude rocket for which he applied and was granted a patent.[14]

The other was a monographical study on legal problems of space activities that he published in German in order to present his legal ideas and

12 *Id.* at 57.

13 Vladimír Mandl, Problém Mezihvězdné Dopravy (The Problem of Interstellar Transport), Praha, 1932.

14 Patent No 52236, class 46 d, granted in Czechoslovakia on September 25, 1933. Mandl also described the design of his rocket in. a brochure Die. Rakete für Höhenforschung (A Rocket for High Altitude Investigation), which was published in Germany by Hachmeister und Thal, 1934, upon request of the then Gesellschaft für fortschrittliche Verkehrstechnik (Association for Progressive Traffic Technics).

conclusions to a wider circle of specialists in Europe. Another reason for it was the fact that he could not find a publisher for such a legal study in Czechoslovakia. But neither was it easy to find any publisher in Germany or elsewhere. Finally, he found a publishing house which, however, agreed only to print Mandl's study at his own cost and to sell it. About 25 copies of the few hundred printed pieces were really sold.[15]

Yet Vladimír Mandl's monographical study on the law of outer space[16] should be assessed as his most significant work, by which its author entered the history of astronautics and particularly that of space law. In this concise study having only 48 pages, he developed a lot of thoughts on the legal regulation of future space activities, some of which have not lost their relevance up to now and are reflected in the present legal regime of outer space. In the framework of this chapter, it is not possible to refer to all of Mandl's ideas and visions. But attention must be drawn at least to the most important ones among them.

First of all, it is his fundamental concept of the law of outer space as an independent legal branch based on specific means of space flights and governed by principles different from those of the law of the sea or the law of the air. Although, Mandl did not underestimate the relevance of concepts of other legal regulations, particularly of air law, for analogies in special cases, he stressed the need for a specific regulation of legal problems of astronautics. The real development of space flights since 1957 and the birth and growth of their legal regulation confirmed the validity of Mandl's concept of space law. From this point of view, he then considered in the first part of his study, en-

15 In Czechoslovakia, one of these copies was purchased by the late Dr. Ing. Rudolf Pešek who was since his youth an enthusiast for aviation and rocketry. After World War II he became Professor of Fluid Mechanics at the Czech Technical University of Prague and in 1960, he was appointed one of the Founding Members of the International Academy of Astronautics (IAA) and Chairman of its Section of Engineering Sciences. When writing the above mentioned first paper on Mandl's life and work, V. Kopal used Professor Pešek's copy of Mandl's study.

16 Vladimír Mandl, Rechtsanwalt in Pilsen, Das Weltraumrecht, Ein Problem der Raumfahrt, (The Space Law: A Problem of Space Flights. By Vladimír Mandl, Attorney-at Law in Pilsen), 1932, J. Bensheimer, Mannheim-Berlin-Leipzig.

titled "The Present", selected problems of a civil, criminal and international law nature concerning outer space.

Not less interesting was and still is the second part of the study called "The Future". It is not science-fiction, but a number of serious prognoses, many of which became a reality in our age. For example, Mandl rejected the then dominant idea of sovereignty in space without limits and affirmed that sovereignty of States applied only to the atmospheric space above their territory. Beyond the territorial spaces, "there begins an area, which does not have any relation to our globe and therefore, also not to any individual part of the Earth's surface, which is no longer Earth appurtenant and is therefore, free of any terrestrial State power, *coelum liberum*. In this area, the traffic of spaceships is completely free."[17]

It is evident that this conclusion of Mandl was inspired by Hugo Grotius and his concept of the freedom of the high seas as defended in his famous "*Mare liberum*" in the beginning of the 17th century.[18] Thirty years after the publication of Mandl's space law study, the UN General Assembly unanimously declared in its Resolution 1721 A/XVI of December 20, 1961 such a principle as the starting point of the space legislation by stating: "Outer space and celestial bodies are free for exploration and use by all States in conformity with international law and are not subject to national appropriation."[19] And only a few years later, this fundamental principle was further developed and made legally binding in Articles I-III of the Outer Space Treaty of January 27, 1967.[20]

In his study Mandl discussed in greater detail many space law notions and questions, such as the nationality of spaceships, the construction of ports in outer space, economic exploration of space resources, effects of space activities on culture and other topics. He also paid attention to the use of spaceships in war, but he expected that "spaceships for a time of war will only be

17 *Id.* at 33.

18 Hugonis Grotii, *Mare Liberum sive de Iure quod Batavis Competit ad Indicana Commercia*, Dissertatio, 1608, in: J.B. Scott, *The Freedom of the Seas*, New York, 1916, especially Chapter V.

19 United Nations Treaties and Principles on Outer Space, United Nations, New York, 2008, p. 61.

20 *Id.* at 4. 21.

used as auxiliary means to the land, sea or air warfares without forming an independent weapon system".[21] Therefore, he did not discuss the possibility of "star wars".

The concluding part of Mandl's considerations was preceded by his prediction of a new surprising progress in physics, chemistry and engineering, which would correspond to a similar epoch of the 19th century – in fact a vision of the scientific and technical revolution of our times.[22] Moreover, as a consequence of the penetration of mankind into outer space, Mandl envisaged a substantive change of relations between the State and its nationals, which would not be based on State domination, so that both the State and its nationals would become equal subjects. According to his vision, the territory will lose its importance as one of the basic elements of each State and new national communities consisting of personal elements only will emerge. People will retain such new nationality when going to outer space and other planets. Mandl was convinced that "no earthly State will be in a position to exercise an organized control over another celestial body in order to bring into effect its laws there; the legal control will thus be illusory and indeed, not only in that distant region but also on the Earth itself."[23] This expectation, Mandl formulated in a concise sentence: "The individual will achieve a legal recognition of his self-determination."[24] And the term space law will become "not only a complex of norms newly added to the existing law, but finally a new set of norms which will be quite a different phenomenon than is the present legal order."[25]

E. Mandl's Other Publications and University Teaching

In 1936, Mandl published in Germany a tiny theoretical study on causal theory of law.[26] In this study Mandl entered the field of theory of law and legal phi-

21 Vladimír Mandl, Das Weltraumrecht, p. 34.

22 *Id.* at 38.

23 *Id.* at 43.

24 *Id.* at 45.

25 *Id.* at 48.

26 Vladimír Mandl, *Eine kausale Rechtstheorie* (A Causal Theory of Law), in: Rechtswissenschaftliche Studien, Heft 60, Verlag Dr. Emil Ebering, Berlin, 1936. In 1938, Mandl also published a Czech version of this study in Prague.

losophy. He considered human economic activities to be the leading momentum of emergence of legal rules and their regulation the utmost purpose. In his opinion, law is a "system of principles which are used by the public power in order to achieve specific socio-economical aims".[27] These principles should be understood as imperatives to pursuit of a specific aim, accompanied by sanctions in the form of psychical pressure. Every legal order is inevitably based on authority, not on physical violation and force.

In the chapter "Law and Society" Mandl then analysed the role of law in various socio-economical periods. He observed the phenomenon of revolutions, which "apparently turn all principles of the former legal order upside down".[28] However, he was skeptical towards the power of revolutionary novelties in legal systems. In his opinion, they represented only a relabeling of the elements of the old legal order.

According to his view expressed in his publication, the role of international law should not be exaggerated: As a system, it is too fragmented to unify all spheres of the national legal order; moreover, international legal norms cannot be enforced because international law lacks any enforcement structure comparable to those of States. Mandl also drew attention to the problem of justice of legal rules: Any legal order has to comply with social flows; positive law as such cannot achieve social justice.

For the purposes of this chapter on Mandl's life and work, the most interesting is "The Supplement" to its study in which the author discussed the consequences of the new phenomenon of his period, the industrialization of human activities. He predicted that the "repeatibility" of human behavior would enable to intensify the application of the principle of causality in the jurisprudence: in contrast thereto, the individuality of human behavior and metaphysical criteria will lose their weight. Only the powers of the legal system, which require and lead to specific behavior of human beings will remain untouched and the law will preserve its character as a mechanism of legal forces and institutions.

Moreover, during the second half of the 1930s, Mandl explained his economic and philosophical views in a number of papers mostly published in

27 *Id.* at 11.

28 *Id.* at 20.

Czechoslovak scientific journals. They offer evidence of his wide erudition and sociological interests.[29]

Starting from the academic year 1933-34, Professor Mandl was lecturing at the same time his course on the law of industrial enterprises at the Czech Technical University in Prague. His last lectures were announced in the University *curricula* for the academic year 1938-39. In September 1938, the four powers (Nazi Germany, Fascist Italy, Great Britain and France) "adjudicated" by the so-called Munich Agreement the frontier regions of Czechoslovakia populated mostly by its German minority to Nazi Germany. And on March 15, 1939 its troops invaded the remaining Czech part of Czechoslovakia. A few months later, in November of the same year, all Czech universities were closed by the occupants as a sanction against the protests of Czech students against the occupation. Thus, the university teaching of Professor Mandl was also terminated.

For some time, Mandl continued his participation in the then efforts of Czech scholars and engineers to finalize the establishing of a National Technical Museum in Prague by search of documents and collection of objects for its aeronautical part, which started during the second half of the 1930s. At that period, Mandl still managed to visit and report on the foreign air collections, such as the Air Museum in Moscow (in 1937) and the Smithsonian Institution in Washington (in 1938). He was also familiar with the aeronautical collections in Paris and Munich. He was still thinking about the aeronautical collection to be established in Prague during his "unvoluntary holidays", as he called it in a handwritten letter dated September 22, 1940, which was addressed to the main organizer of the collection from the tuberculosis sanatorium in Pleš near Prague, when his health condition was deteriorating.

29 He did so e.g. in the following papers: *Technokracie, hospodářský systém budoucnosti* (Technocracy – Economic System of the Future), Prague, 1934; *Přírodovědní národohospodářská teorie* (Scientific Economic Theory), Prague, 1936; *Stát a vědecká organizace práce* (State and Scientific Management of Labour), Pilsen, 1937. From among his other papers the following studies should be mentioned: *Vědecká metoda Einsteinova relativismu* (Scientific Method of Einstein's Relativity) in Česká mysl, časopis filosofický (Czech Thought, a Philosophical Journal), Vol. 31, No. 3-4, Prague, 1915. On the eve of World War II, Mandl published a study entitled *Válka a mír* (War and Peace), Prague, 1938.

On January 8, 1941 Vladimír Mandl died in his uncompleted forty-second year and was buried in the Mandl family tomb at the Central Cemetery of Pilsen, in the city where he had been born and spent most of his life.

F. Evaluation of Mandl's Work in Space Legal Literature

Vladimír Mandl was the first author who approached future legal problems of space flights as a legal scholar. He attempted to create a system of ideas and legal principles to govern activities in outer space 25 years before such activities started and the process of establishing the rule of law for this vast area was initiated.

Several later authors specializing in this newly born discipline of space law recognized his fundamental role in creating its doctrine. For example, Dr. Welf-Heinrich Prinz von Hannover, in his doctoral thesis that he defended at the University of Göttingen (Germany), mentioned Mandl as the first among the early writers on space law.[30] Ernst Fasan (Austria), Honorary Director of the International Institute of Space Law (IISL), called Mandl "The Father of Space Law" in his monograph on this subject.[31] Gerhard Reintanz, former Professor of the Martin Luther University in Halle/Saale (Germany), appreciated Mandl as "one of the pioneers of Space Law" who should not be forgotten.[32] Stephan Hobe, Director of the Institute of Air and Space Law, University of Cologne (Germany) and Director of Studies of the IISL, precisely summarized Mandl's work with special attention to Mandl's 1932 space law study in his above mentioned report on early writers on space law that he presented at the 2010 Colloquium of the IISL which he concluded: "The work of Vladimír Mandl is so impressive because it was so early and so informed when he wrote about space flight and space law …. An expert in air law, in

30 The English translation of Prinz von Hannover's thesis Air Law and Space Law was later printed in Legal Problems of Space Exploration, A Symposium, prepared for the use of the Committee on Aeronautical and Space Sciences of the US Senate, Washington, D.C., 1961, p. 271 *et seq.*

31 Ernst Fasan, Weltraumrecht (Space Law), Mainz, 1965, p. 21.

32 Gerhard Reintanz, *Vladimír Mandl – The Father of Space Law*, in: Proceedings of the Eleventh Colloquium of the Law of Outer Space, International Institute of Space Law of the IAF, October 17-18, 1968, p. 365.

German marriage law, and other fields of law, he is also very knowledgeable in space science, rocket technology, and offers, in 1932, a tremendously innovative study".[33]

Finally, Stephen E. Doyle (USA), Honorary Director of the IISL, who devoted a great effort to the research into the history of space law, should be quoted in the conclusion of this chapter on Vladimír Mandl: "Mandl was clearly a man of genius. He died at the relatively young age of 41, having done and produced more work in his lifetime than many could accomplish in twice his life's span.... Mandl's extrapolation of future relations among humans in a different society and relations between them and their institutions is a speculative, visionary, courageous and philosophical piece of writing. This young lawyer, engineer, pilot, professor, inventor, was also a remarkable philosopher. His work deserves more study than it has received. Mandl's writing will repay serious effort devoted to its study with many rewards."[34]

It must be regretted that due to his premature passing away, Vladimír Mandl could not witness and comment on the accomplishment of the first space flights, the landing on the Moon, the establishment of the first space stations and the development of international cooperation in space activities, as well as to participate in the creation of the peaceful regime for outer space.

33 Stephan Hobe, *Vladimír Mandl, Alex Mayer, Welf-Heinrich, Prince of Hannover, Friedrich Wilhelm von Rauchhaupt. Early Writings in German on the Young Discipline of Space Law*, in: Proceedings of the International Institute of Space Law, 2010, p. 21 *et seq.*

34 Stephen E. Doyle, Concepts of Space Law Before Sputnik, 2009, the manuscript of a major historical work so far unpublished, pp. 107-108. The authors of this chapter borrowed the relevant parts of Dr. Doyle's work from him and quote them with his permission. Upon his initiative, a translation of Mandl's study on Space Law into English was provided by Lloyd E. Jonas, Jr. Subsequently, the US Aeronautics and Space Administration (NASA) sponsored a new translation of Mandl's study, which was completed in 1984. The first translator was then requested to reconcile the substantive and stylistic differences between the two translations. Dr. Doyle considers this emerging text as "the best translation that could be made half a century after the original author's death." (*Id.* at 58) The authors of the present chapter used it for interpreting Mandl´s original German text, which was juridically correct and precise, but they applied some own translations in the relevant quotations.

G. Bibliography of the Main Works of Vladimír Mandl

1. Letecké právo (Air Law), Plzeň, 1928.

2. Automobilový zákon z. 9. Srpna 1908 A Jeho Reforma (The Automobile Act of August 9, 1908 and its Reform), Praha, 1929.

3. Mezinárodní Úmluva O Úpravě Letectví Ze Dne 13. Října 1919 (International Convention on the Regulation of Aviation of October 13, 1919), Praha, 1932.

4. Zivilistischer Aufbau des Schadenersatzrechtes, Breslau, 1932.

5. Problém Mezihvězdné Dopravy (The Problem of Interstellar Transport), Praha, 1932.

6. Das Weltraum-Recht: Ein Problem der Raumfahrt, Mannheim – Berlin – Leipzig, 1932.

7. Die Rakete zur Höhenforschung – ein Beitrag zum Raumfahrtproblem (The Rocket for the Exploration of Great Heights – A Contribution to the Problem of Spaceflight), Leipzig – Berlin, 1934.

8. Technokracie, Hospodářský Systém Budoucnosti (Technocracy – Economic System of the Future), Praha, 1934.

9. Přírodovědní Národohospodářská Teorie (Natural Science Economic Theory), Praha, 1936.

10. Essays Of A European Technocrat, Los Angeles, 1936.

11. Eine kausale Rechtstheorie, Rechtswissenschaftliche Studien, Heft 60, Berlin, 1936.

12. Stát A Vědecká Organizace Práce (State and Scientific Management of Labour), Plzeň, 1937.

13. Válka A Mír (War and Peace), Praha, 1938.

Chapter VI **Andrew G. Haley** (4.11.1904 – 10.9.1966)

Stephen E. Doyle*

A. Introduction

Andrew G. Haley was one of the world's first practicing space lawyers. Emile Laude had written the first article mentioning space law in 1910. Vladimir Mandl had published the first monograph describing space law in 1932. Welf Heinrich Prince of Hannover, wrote the first doctoral dissertation on space law, but Haley was among those who first brought the practice of law to the needs and problems of astronautics. The pathways he travelled in becoming a world renowned space lawyer were numerous, complex paths, with many surprising intersections, and strewn with many unique accomplishments.

In 1942 Haley led a small group of rocketeers in the formation of a business venture to begin early commercial production of rockets in the United States. He was later directed to lead that organization (Aerojet Engineering Corporation) as President, which he did through years of the Second World War (1942-45). Following the war, Haley returned to practice law in Washington, DC, and he subsequently served as General Counsel of the American Rocket Society (ARS) (1950-1963), as Director of the Society (1951-52), as ARS Vice President (1953-54), as President (1954-55) and as Chairman of the Board (1956-57). Haley also served the International Astronautical Federation as a Vice President (1951-54), Chairman, International Affairs Committee (1953-57), President (1957-59) and as a member of the Federation's governing Bureau and General Counsel (1959-61).

* Honorary Director, International Institute of Space Law.

Stephan Hobe (ed.), Pioneers of Space Law
 ISBN 978-90-04-24027-8. pp. 71-97

The most important, constructive, and visionary of his accomplishments concerning space law was the early work in which Haley urged and promoted the international establishment of dedicated radio frequencies to support spaceflight development from its earliest days. Trained as a lawyer, experienced in the development of radio and the relevant regulatory communications law, Haley could see sooner and far more clearly than many around him the important, enabling role radio must play in astronautics. Having engaged in many early practices of space law, later Haley was centrally involved in the creation of the International Astronautical Federation (1951-52), the International Academy of Astronautics (1960), and the International Institute of Space Law (1960). Thereafter, for the six years until his death in 1966, Haley was a prolific speaker and writer continuing to produce books, articles, papers and commentary describing and recommending many aspects of the then emerging space law.

B. Childhood

Andrew Gallagher Haley was born in Tacoma, Washington, on November 4, 1904. He was the sixth of nine children. He had 5 sisters and 3 brothers. In 1906 his family moved to Seattle, Washington, and in 1908 to Olympia, Washington. His father was a trained engineer and an artisan in production of wooden pipes, widely used for water and sewage in the first quarter of the 20th century. Haley's grade school education included time in Vancouver, British Columbia, but was completed in Tacoma, Washington. As a young boy he was deeply impressed by frequent talks with a neighboring retired professor of astronomy, who piqued young Andrew's interest in the moon, the planets, the stars and the cosmos. Andrew's older brother Christopher wrote: "Through the years of grade school and high school [1910-1922], Andy entertained his teachers and his fellow students with his fictional writings of outer space. Many of the things he wrote about in those early years later became reality."[1]

While an energetic, blue-eyed teenager in high school, Haley was employed from the age of 14 after school hours by the *Tacoma News Tribune*, a

1 C. Thomas Haley, *Great Grandfather Tells All*, p. 40, a personal memoir produced for family members, 1981.

daily newspaper. He exhibited a great versatility there, working in circulation, manning the telephone switchboard at night, writing about local high school activities, and working on the city desk covering general news, police and court activities. Encouraged by the publisher of the paper, he became a regular contributor to the newspaper. This was valuable experience supporting this future hortatory writing and reporting concerning space law. While employed at the newspaper, 1919-1922, Haley met several congressmen and senators whose lives in politics were to influence his future education and career.[2]

C. Education and Marriage

In 1923, aged 19, Haley went to Washington, D. C., to seek his education at Georgetown University. While studying Haley became engaged in politics, serving as a staff member of the Democratic National Campaign Committee in 1924. After two parallel years of undergraduate studies and four years of law school he received an LL. B. degree from Georgetown University in 1928. That year he returned to Tacoma and practiced law there from 1929 to 1932. He then returned to Washington, DC and entered George Washington University, receiving a B. A. degree there in 1934.

While at Georgetown University, he served as a post graduate research associate in public international law to Prof. James Brown Scott (1927-28). He also earned a certificate for studies in international law and historical jurisprudence from Cambridge University in England. After returning to Tacoma in 1928, he served as a staff assistant to the General Manager of the Pacific Telephone and Telegraph Company in 1929, then as a secretary to Congressman Ralph Horr, 1931-32. Haley returned to Washington, D. C. as administrative assist to Congressman Wesley Lloyd (1932-33). In 1933 he was appointed an attorney in the Federal Radio Commission. In 1934 he married Delphine Delacroix of Mobile, Alabama, and the couple had two children, Delphine Delacroix (1936) and Andrew Gallagher Jr. (1938).[3] Haley's younger sister, Margaret, died when a young woman leaving two children, Andrew

2 "Our Respects to Andrew Gallagher Haley", *Broadcasting*, Nov. 11, 1957, Wash., D. C.

3 *Id.* and *see* Shirley Thomas, *Men of Space*, Volume 7, 139, Chilton Books, Philadelphia, 1965.

and Mary Michaela Voigt. Haley adopted these two children to be raised with his own.[4]

D. Learning Communications Law

Through his political acquaintances Haley was able to obtain part-time and supporting roles in selected congressional activities. While a student at Georgetown University, he did research for US Senator C. C. Dill in drafting the Federal Radio Act of 1927, and similarly assisted in the drafting of the successor Communications Act of 1934. As noted earlier, in 1933 Haley was appointed an attorney in the Federal Radio Commission, and in 1934 in the successor Federal Communications Commission. He served as an attorney in these federal regulatory agencies from 1933 to 1939.[5] In 1939 Haley joined with W. Theodore (Ted) Pearson (another FCC attorney) to establish a private law practice specializing in communications and federal administrative law. He remained in Washington, D. C. in private law practice until the US entered the Second World War, when he entered military service in 1941. In early 1942 he served as chief of the military affairs division in the Office of the Air Judge Advocate of the US Army Air Corps. Haley's military service was cut short in 1942, when General H. H. Arnold, Commander of the US Army Air Corps, decided Haley's talents would be more valuable to the US war effort in an industrial management role.[6]

E. Entering the World of Rocketeers

World renowned aerodynamicist, Theodore von Kármán, contemplated creating a rocket manufacturing firm with a few colleagues. Von Kármán wrote

4 *Id.*

5 Some of Haley's publications during this period included; A. G. Haley, "Radio law – Broadcast-ing and the Public Interest Involved", *Georgetown L. J.*, 1-27, May, 1934; "The Broadcasting and Postal Lottery Statutes', *Geo. Wash. L. R.*, 475-496, 1936; reprinted as U. S. Congress, 75th Cong., 3rd Sess., Senate Doc. No. 137, USGPO, Jan. 1937.

6 T. von Kármán and L. Edson, *The Wind and Beyond: Theodore von Kármán*, 257, Little, Brown and Co., Boston, 1967.

in his biography: "In January and February 1942, [Frank] Malina, [Andrew] Haley, [Martin] Summerfield, [Ed] Forman, [John] Parsons and I met in the living room of my home to lay the foundations of our rocket company. To show our seriousness of purpose we agreed to put up two hundred dollars a piece. This I might say was a considerable gamble in those days for a theoretical professor, his former graduate students, and two young rocket tinkerers – only Haley had business experience."[7] Von Kármán also reported that on March 19, 1942, Haley registered with the government the incorporation papers by which Aerojet Engineering Corporation was created.[8] Haley initially assumed the position of Aerojet Corporate Secretary, and returned to Washington, leaving the fledgling company in the hands of President von Kármán, three Vice Presidents: Forman, Parsons and Summerfield, and Treasurer Malina. According to von Kármán's biography, after a few months the army contracting office issued a stop work order on a contract in process at Aerojet, because of inadequate management of the resources being provided by the Aerojet. Von Kármán petitioned Gen. Arnold to assist him by providing competent management skills to help run the company. Before nightfall that same day, Haley was relieved from active duty in the Air Judge Advocate's office to permit him to accept the position of President of Aerojet Engineering Corporation in California.[9]

F. Industrial Leader

There are numerous descriptions of Haley's impacts on the organization, staffing, and performance of the company.[10] Under von Kármán's and Frank Malina's leadership the technical work proceeded well at Aerojet, but the business management and record keeping were given little attention. In the spring of 1942, when Army auditors discovered Aerojet's slipshod record keeping, von Kármán was directed to stop work. The installation of Haley as

7 *Id.*

8 *Id.* at 259.

9 *Id.*

10 As Examples, *see* Thomas, *Men of Space*, 140-142, *op. cit. supra*, note 3; Von Kármán, *the Wind and Beyond*, 256-260, *op. cit. supra*, note 6; and A. G. Haley, *Rocketry and Space Exploration*, 157-158, D. van Nostrand Co., Princeton, 1958.

President provided the confidence required by the Army contracting office to allow Aerojet to resume work under its contract. Haley became President and General Manager of Aerojet Engineering on August 26, 1942,[11] serving in that role until 1945. While managing Aerojet, Haley lectured in 1943 at the first Jet Propulsion School in the US, set up by the military. The contracts at Aerojet multiplied, and Haley managed the challenges of moving to more capacious facilities and a constantly expanding work force, which were required to meet the expanding work requirements.

Haley wrote of this period: "It soon became apparent that, in order to do the job envisioned [for Aerojet] by the Armed Services, the company would require adequate testing grounds. A site was selected by Haley at Azusa, California, and he was able to obtain Defense Plant Corporation financing for most of this project. However, the dollar volume of the contracts for liquid and solid propellant JATO units and for many other developments, including items of basic research, mounted so fast that it was quite impossible for the financial authorities in the Army and Navy Departments continuously to provide what amounted to almost 100% financing of the operations of the company."[12]

In 1944 defense contracting officials told Haley they could not continue granting to Aerojet programs involving millions of dollars when the company did not have the basic 10% of its own capital with which to perform the contracts. Because of the classified confidential and secret nature of many Aerojet contracts, the company was not at liberty to discuss its business matters with potential investors to gain their confidence for investment. Haley persisted and finally obtained permission to discuss possible investment with a former client of his Washington, D. C. law firm, the General Tire and Rubber Company. When approached, with DoD permission, that company agreed to invest in Aerojet, and eventually purchased stock enough to assume control of the company in 1945 as Aerojet General, but they decided to retain the key leadership in place and the work force recruited and trained under von Kármán, Malina, Summerfield and Haley.[13]

11 Von Kármán, *the Wind and Beyond,* 259, *op. cit. supra,* note 6.

12 A. G. Haley, *Rocketry and Space Exploration,* 157, *op. cit. supra,* note 10.

13 *Id.* at 158.

In August 1945 Haley resigned his positions as President and a Director of the Aerojet Engineering Corporation to return to Washington, D. C. Immediately following his resignation he was appointed Adviser on Aircraft to the US Senate Subcommittee on Aviation and Light Metals of the Special Senate Committee to Investigate the National Defense Program, which held hearings on the post-war problems of restructuring (reconversion) and the future of the aviation industry in the United States. This work lasted for one year and concluded for Haley in 1947. Haley participated in drafting the final report, which urged the Congress, among other things, to unify the command of the Armed Services and to step up the development of rocketry.

With his continuing interest in radio, Haley served as legal advisor to the 87-nation International Telecommunication Conference in Washington DC, in 1947 and to the 4th Inter-American Radio Conference in Washington, D. C. in 1949. He also served as an industry advisor to the Third North American Regional Broadcasting Conference in Montreal, P. Q., Canada in 1949 and in Havana, Cuba and Washington, D. C. in 1950, and as an industry advisor at the Mexican-United States Broadcasting Conference, Mexico City, 1954 and Washington, D. C., 1956. Although he became increasingly more active in astronautical pursuits, urging development of space law, Haley remained active in his routine practice of communication law, which included occasional appearances before Congress related to international agreements and regulations for broadcasters.[14]

Residing again in Washington, D. C., and having re-entered the practice of law, Haley sustained his contacts with his associations in rocketry

14 As examples, *see* U. S. Congress, Hearings before the Senate Committee on Foreign Affairs, Subcommittee on the North American Regional Broadcasting Agreement and the Mexican Broadcasting Agreement, "Statement of Andrew G. Haley", July 11, 1957, USGPO, Wash., D. C., 1957; and another statement before the same subcommittee on January 24, 1960, 82nd Cong. 2nd Sess., USGPO, Wash., D. C., 1960; U. S. Congress, Hearings before a Subcommittee of the House Committee on Interstate and Foreign Commerce, 86th Cong., 2nd Sess., "Statement of Andrew G. Haley", June 1960, USGPO, Wash., D. C., 1960; and testimony and a statement in U. S. Congress, Hearings before the House Committee on Science and Astronautics, 87th Cong., 2nd Sess., May 10, 1961, USGPO, Wash., D. C., 1961.

by maintaining an active membership and assuming leadership roles in the American Rocket Society (ARS).

G. International Telecommunication Union (ITU)

At the Sixth Colloquium on the Law of Outer Space, convened by the IISL at Paris, France, in September 1963,[15] Kenneth A. Finch presented an excellent primer explaining the role and methods of work of the ITU and a useful description of the results of some early ITU meetings dealing with astronautical radio. The following materials, which present important background to understanding Haley's activities in the latter half of the 1950s, draw heavily from the Finch presentation in 1963.[16]

The ITU is the primary organization in the world for international coordination of electronic communication matters. It deals with telephone, telegraph, and radio communications, setting standards and facilitating international system interconnections and cooperation. In the discharge of its radio regulation responsibilities the ITU works through Administrative Radio Conferences and the International Consultative Committee on Radio, referred to as the CCIR, after its French language initials. The CCIR comprises Study Groups, and these groups develop frequency planning recommendations which are considered from time to time by Administrative Radio Conferences of the Union.

The Union also maintains an International Frequency Registration Board (IFRB), a five member board with the secretariat in Geneva, Switzerland. This board maintains records of the allocation and assignment of all radio frequencies made available for use globally. To maintain order in the use of the radio spectrum it is essential to have specific radio services perform in particular frequency ranges as a means of avoiding interference between different services. The ITU allocates bands of radio frequencies for use by particular services, and the member administrations (national governments) then

15 A. G. Haley (ed.), PROCEEDINGS OF THE SIXTH COLLOQUIUM ON THE LAW OF OUTER SPACE, IISL of the International Astronautical Federation, Paris, France, Sep. 26-28, 1963, unpaginated, Wash., D. C., 1964.

16 K. A. Finch, *"Space Communications: Catalyst for International Understanding"*, *in* PROCEEDINGS OF THE SIXTH COLLOQUIUM ON THE LAW OF OUTER SPACE, *op. cit. supra, note 15.*

license (assign) particular frequencies in an authorized band for use by a particular licensee. All assignments are then reported back to the ITU and are entered into the international frequency register maintained by the IFRB.

H. Organizational Leader

Living in Washington, D. C., Haley gradually assumed roles of increasing organizational management responsibility in the American Rocket Society (ARS). He served as the Society's General Counsel from 1950 to 1963. He served as an ARS Director in 1951-52, and was re-elected a Director for the period 1955-57. He was elected Vice President of the Society in 1953 and President in 1954. In January 1956 he was elected Chairman of the Society's Board of Directors. As early as 1952 the internal work of the ARS began concentrating on the prospects of man-made satellites through the work of the Society's Space Flight Committee. Haley was the initial chairman of the ARS Space Flight Committee. At that time (1952), Haley and other ARS members perceived the need for radio communication use in the conduct and monitoring of spaceflight activities.

Haley was active in parallel with his ARS roles in gradually increasing responsibilities in the IAF. He was elected a Vice President of the IAF in 1951 and served in that role until 1957. He was a co-drafter of the IAF's constitution, and he was an original co-chair and later Chairman of the IAF International Committee during the 1950s. Haley was elected President of the IAF, serving in that position from 1957-59. He also served as IAF General Counsel from 1958 to 1960, which also placed him *ex officio* on the Bureau of the IAF.

In April 1954, Commissioner George E. Sterling of the US Federal Communications Commission in Washington, DC, presented his views to the ARS National Capital Section on needs for regulation of satellite uses of radio. This early, authoritative statement clearly evidenced some US Government concern about the need for rules and regulations related to radio usage in emerging astronautical capabilities. Sterling's short paper did not propose solutions so much as it called attention to emerging issues that would require national and international attention of regulators. The clear global nature and impacts of radio uses in astronautics are repeatedly manifest in the paper. As Commissioner Sterling wrote "I believe that there will be many technical problems as well as regulatory problems associated with communications in connection with rockets that travel far from the Earth. I am not aware of any study which has been made in this regard, but I think it would be a very fruitful field for exploration."[17]

During 1954, on behalf of the ARS, Haley, as President, submitted a proposal prepared by the ARS Space Flight Committee to the National Science Foundation to sponsor a study of "The Utility of an Artificial Unmanned Earth Satellite". The US Armed Services were already at work on this subject in classified studies and the National Science Foundation took no action on the ARS proposal. In December 1954 the ARS presented Haley with a special award – a plaque with the engraving "... in appreciation for distinguished service and untiring efforts on behalf of the Society during his term as President."

As General Counsel in the ARS, Haley was selected in 1951 to represent the ARS at a meeting of several national rocket societies hosted by the British Interplanetary Society in London. This meeting followed the Astronautical Congress organized by Alexandre Ananoff in Paris during September/October 1950. The 1950 Congress, the first of its kind, involved participants from Argentina, Austria, Denmark, Federal Republic of Germany, France, Great Britain, Spain and Sweden. The group agreed in 1950 to meet again in London in 1951 to continue discussing creation of an international astronautical organization.

In 1951 there were several American rocket organizations represented at the astronautical meeting in London, including the ARS, represented by Haley, the Detroit Rocket Society, the Pacific Rocket Society and the Reaction Research Society. Representatives also participated from Argentina, Austria, Federal Republic of Germany, France, Great Britain, Italy, the Netherlands, Spain, Sweden and Switzerland. This meeting decided to create the International Astronautical Federation (IAF).[18] A Secretariat was authorized to form in Switzerland under elected Secretary Joseph Stemmer (Swiss). Eugene Sänger (Austria) was elected President, and Gunter Löser (FRG) and

17 Sterling, G. E., "Utilization of Radio Frequencies in Connection with Rockets," *Jet Propulsion*, vol. 24, no. 5, Sep. – Oct. 1954, 322-23.

18 *See* http://www.iafastro.com/index.html?title=History (last visited July 5, 2012); also A. G, Haley, *Rocketry and Space Exploration* 230, *op. cit. supra* note 10; and L. R. Shepherd, "The International Astronautical Federation", vol.1, no. 5, *Spaceflight*, 159-163, London.

Andrew Haley (US) were elected Vice Presidents. From this date forward Haley served tirelessly in attempting to gain recognition of the IAF by other international organizations, including the International Council of Scientific Unions (ICSU), the United Nations Educational, Scientific and Cultural Organization (UNESCO), and the International Telecommunication Union (ITU). Haley has recorded fully and faithfully his sustained roles and diligent activities in promoting the interests of the IAF.[19]

While serving in increasingly senior management positions in the ARS and the IAF, Haley undertook a sustained campaign to urge and convince the US Government and the International Telecommunication Union to initiate and pursue international consideration of the needs of astronautics for internationally agreed, dedicated radio frequencies, which are essential to the effective conduct of spaceflight. The following chronological summary of activities demonstrates how committed and persistent Haley was in this developing period of radio regulation for astronautics.

Speaking to the 75th Annual Convention of the Tennessee Bar Association in June 1956 Haley noted that as spaceflight activities approached "... science and government must advance more rapidly in the field or telecommunications than in any other field. Fortunately, a great deal of the management machinery is already set up in the various agencies of the International Telecommunication Union and through the cooperative arrangements with the United Nations."[20] It is one thing to have a resource available; it is another to make timely and effective use of the resource. Haley recommended that the existing machinery be used:

(1) To undertake a study in the CCIR of the communication requirements of contact with and remote control of manned and unmanned earth satellites and vehicles traveling beyond the aeropause.

(2) To ask the International Frequency Registration Board (IFRB of the ITU) to advise the CCIR what frequency bands might be available to meet such requirements.

19 A. G, Haley, *Rocketry and Space Exploration* 229-237, *op. cit. supra* note 10.

20 A. G. Haley, "Space Law – Basic Concepts", 24 *Tenn. Law Rev.* 643 (1956), reprinted in 6 *L. Rev. Digest* 71 (1956).

(3) To exchange representatives at UNESCO and meetings discussing use of radio for earth satellites and spaceflight.
(4) Following these initial steps, the ITU should convene formal proceedings to allocate frequencies internationally for remote control of and communication with space vehicles.[21]

A similar set of proposals had been sent to the ITU by Haley in a letter on behalf of the IAF to the ITU Secretary-General, Aurelio Marco Andrada on April 16, 1956. That letter contained the four points presented in Haley's Tennessee speech, with a fifth point: namely, that the IAF should be allowed to send representatives to the appropriate meetings of the CCIR and the IFRB.[22] The ITU responded on June 11, 1956 informing Haley that the ITU considered the matters presented in the April 16 letter as appropriate for the administration of individual member nations.[23] The IAF believed that the issues raised could not be resolved effectively by actions of individual nations. Haley renewed the IAF's proposals to the ITU and while pursuing status to work in the ITU, he initiated proposals to the US Federal Communications Commission (FCC). On behalf of the ARS Haley submitted proposals in a series of administrative rule-making procedures as the FCC prepared itself to participate, with the Department of State, in the frequency planning and allocation work of the ITU.

During the September 1956 Warsaw meeting of the CCIR, Haley wrote on behalf of the IAF to Professor Balth de Pol, Director of the CCIR. In this letter the IAF reviewed progress to date in development of Earth orbiting satellites and in planning for cislunar and circumlunar space vehicles, highlighting the importance of radio communications for guidance of such spaceflight activities. The IAF urged that the CCIR was the only international body capable to study and regulate globally the subjects of astronautical radio communications, and urged appropriate study be completed so that a report could be

21 *Id.*

22 *See* the account *in* A. G. Haley, "Space Age Radio Frequency Allocation", *Astronautics & Aeronautics*, May 1966. *See* also A. G. Haley, "The International Astronautical Federation and Space Communications", Remarks before the Delegates to the Administrative Radio Conference of the ITU, Geneva, Oct., 1959.

23 *Id.*

rendered to the ITU Administrative Radio Conference planned for Geneva in 1959.[24]

Acting as General Counsel of the ARS and Vice President of the IAF, in 1956 Haley attended the VIIIth Plenary Assembly of the International Consultative Committee on Radio (CCIR) of the ITU, August to September 1956, in Warsaw, Poland. There he presented a proposed plan to accommodate clearly emerging astronautical radio needs. In July 1956 both the United States and Soviet Union had announced their intentions to establish earth orbiting satellites to support the scientific work of the International Geophysical Year (IGY), which would extend from July I, 1957 to December 31, 1958. There were at that time no allocated frequencies reserved for spaceflight radio activities. On 13 September, 1956, at its 13th Plenary Meeting in Warsaw, the CCIR authorized its Director to invite the IAF to apply for membership in the CCIR. With support from the ITU's Deputy Secretary-General, Gerald Gross, the IAF sought association with the ITU on May 10, 1957. The ITU Administrative Council Meeting in May 1957, decided to include the IAF in the list of international organizations to be notified of the planned 1959 ITU Administrative Radio Conference in Geneva, and authorized IAF participation in that meeting.

Haley was able to meet and talk with Dr. E. Metzler, who was elected Director of the CCIR at the end of the 1956 Warsaw meeting. Constructive technical interchanges were held during which Haley was able to explain to Dr. Metzler the need for and importance of early action on frequency allocations by the ITU. Later in 1956, as noted above, in collaboration with the Assistant Secretary-General of the ITU, Dr. Metzler was able to arrange observer status for the IAF at subsequent ITU meetings. According to Haley "This achievement actually was due to the sympathetic leadership of the Department of State's mission [to the UN in Geneva], and to help from Washington, particularly from Mr. [Francis Colt] DeWolf [in the Office of Telecommunication Policy, Bureau of Economic Affairs, Department of State]."[25]

24 *Id.*

25 Letter from Andrew G. Haley, General Counsel, IAF, to Ralph a Jones, Deputy Director, Soviet and Eastern European Affairs, Department of State, dated May 22, 1961; copies in A. G. Haley files, National Center for Remote Sensing, Air, and Space Law, University of Mississippi.

In April 1957 the FCC released a Notice of Inquiry (first step in a formal rule-making) to examine the most desirable and appropriate allocation of frequencies in the radio spectrum between 25 and 890 megacycles (Mc/s) (FCC Docket No. 11997). On November 25, 1957 the ARS filed a first round of formal comments in this proceeding proposing for the first time in the US that radio frequencies be allocated for use in communications from Earth to vehicles in space, and for communications between stations on Earth and places or objects in space. The ARS advised the FCC that frequency requirements existed at that time in the frequency band below 200 Mc/s, in the 400-600 Mc/s range, and in other portions of the spectrum. The ARS filed subsequent comments in this same docket on October 31, 1958, and on April 3, 1959.

In late 1957 the FCC also issued a Notice of Inquiry in Docket No. 12263, intended to elicit information from the public and industry to help prepare for participation in the planned Administrative Radio Conference in Geneva in 1959. On January 23, 1958 the ARS filed comments in this proceeding proposing that the FCC create new radio services for an Astronautical Mobile Service, an Astronautical Radiolocation Service, an Astronautical Radionavigation Service and authority for stations to operate in each service. Multiple specific frequencies were proposed to be allocated in 14 separate radio frequency bands. These bands were proposed by the IAF to the CCIR's Study Group XI meeting in Moscow later in 1958.

While serving in management roles in the American Rocket Society and in the management of affairs of the International Astronautical Federation, Haley took the time during the summer and fall of 1957 to organize and participate in a two major tours. Travelling with Welf Heinrich, Prince of Hanover, Haley toured in the United States and Europe speaking at more than 30 universities and at dozens of professional organizations about the emerging law to stimulate interest in space law. Welf Heinrich, author of the world's first doctoral dissertation on space law,[26] has written a memoir about

26 Hannover, W.H., *Air Law and Space*, translated and reproduced in the *Saint Louis University Law Journal*, Spring 1958, 11-69; reproduced in U. S. Congress, *Space Law: A Symposium*, prepared at the request of Lyndon B. Johnson, Chairman, Senate Special Committee on Space and Astronautics, 85th Cong., 2nd Sess., Committee Print, GPO, Wash., DC, Dec. 31, 1958, 18-76.

his experience traveling and lecturing with Haley.[27]

An Extended Session of the CCIR Study Group XI was held in Moscow during May-June 1958. Haley participated on behalf of the IAF. At that meeting the US Delegation advanced the cause of astronautical radio, and at that meeting a formal CCIR study program was agreed. The United States Committee for CCIR Study Group VI drafted a proposed new question for study: "Protection of Frequencies used by Artificial Earth Satellites or Other Space Vehicles for Communication and Position Observation." Sessions of CCIR Study Groups V and VII took place in August 1958 in Geneva. On behalf of the IAF Haley also submitted a proposal for relevant studies to those meetings.

Sputnik was launched by the Soviet Union on October 4, 1957. By that time the US had further considered the studies proposed at the previous meetings of the CCIR Study Groups V and VI. The US obtained co-sponsor signatures from 14 nations on a proposal for further study which was certified for consideration at the forthcoming CCIR Plenary Session to be held in Los Angeles in April 1959. As a result of deliberations at Los Angeles, the US delegation was successful in having the entire mix of issues involved in astronautical radio considered in detail at the ITU Administrative Radio Conference held in Geneva from August to December 1959. At the 10th Annual Congress of the IAF in London in September 1959 Haley had been directed to present the views of the IAF at the Geneva meeting. Haley participated in Geneva on behalf of the IAF and as an advisor to the US Delegation.[28]

A subsequent commentator on the significance of the Administrative Radio Conference (ARC), Geneva (1959) noted that "...it was an important event for space telecommunications. For the first time a 'space service' was established by the Regulations, and frequencies were allocated for this serv-

27 A paper entitled "Law of the Space Age" was presented in two parts: Part 1 by Heinrich and Part 2 by Haley. *See* Hannover, W.H., *"Eine Reise in Sachen ,Weltraumrecht,' Eindrücke und Erlebnisse einer Vortragsreise durch die Staaten von Amerika im Jahre 1957"* (A Trip on the Matter of Space Law, Impressions and Experiences of a Speaking Tour in the American States in 1957), *in Beiträge zum Luft- und Weltraumrecht; Festschrift zu Ehren von Alex Meyer,* Carl Heymanns Verlag KG, Köln, 1975, 385-395. *See* also the brief notice about this trip in *Astronautics,* November 1957, 88.

28 *See* sources cited at note 22, above.

ice on a shared channel basis."[29] Milton Smith went on to note that "While these allocations were for space research purposes only, the launch of Sputnik in 1957 and subsequent satellite launches, demonstrated that demands on the radio spectrum would increase rapidly." Smith also noted that the 1959 ARC in Geneva adopted a Recommendation "to hold a conference in 1963 to allocate additional frequency bands for space purposes, if warranted by technological progress."[30]

As a result of deliberations in Geneva, selected frequencies were identified for limited astronautical research uses, and the uses were to be on a shared basis. Mindful of the progress in spaceflight occurring in the USSR and the US, the conference agreed to schedule an Extraordinary Administrative Radio Conference (EARC) of the ITU in 1963 for consideration of astronautical radio uses. A detailed proposal entitled "A Basic Program for the 1963 Extraordinary Administrative Radio Conference on Space Communications" was prepared by Haley on behalf of the IAF and submitted at the beginning of the 1963 conference. Conferees deliberated, discussed and negotiated all the various national proposals submitted for one month.

The EARC made allocations for communications, meteorological and navigational satellites, for space research, radioastronomy, and the application of space techniques in the aviation radio and amateur radio services. In addition provisions were made for support functions including space telemetering, tracking, and telecommand. The conference set procedures for the international notification by member administrations for registration of individual frequency assignments brought into service for these newly authorized services. The conference also established technical criteria for frequency sharing between terrestrial and space radio services on an equitable basis.[31] The conference ended on November 8, 1963 having established a partial revision of the Radio Regulations (Geneva 1959), with annexes and an additional

29 Milton L. Smith, *International Regulation of Satellite Communications*, 59, Martinus Nijhoff, Dordrecht, 1990.

30 *Id.*

31 U. S. Congress, Senate Committee on Foreign Relations, *Partial Revision of the Radio Regulations (Geneva 1959) and Additional Protocols*, a message from the President of the U. S. transmitting the adopted revisions for advice and consent, 88th Cong., 1st Sess., Senate Executive Document, transmittal dated Dec. 16, 1963 at 2.

protocol, signed by participating delegations at Geneva. The Secretary of State, Dean Rusk, submitting the conference's Final Acts for Congressional approval, urged: "In the interest of continued U. S. space leadership it is considered important that this country move forward quickly with ratification of the final acts of this Conference."[32]

Andrew Haley had initiated consideration of space radio needs within the ARS in 1952, and recommended a major national study of the need for space radio regulations by the National Science Foundation in 1954. He inaugurated considerations of space radio in the CCIR in the mid-1950s and sustained that effort, through the national structure of the FCC and continually in the study group activities of the CCIR, and ultimately the ITU through the 1950s. Haley's footprints on the international pathway to space radio regulations were early and significant, and few if any individuals brought as much vision, energy, creativity and determination to satisfying the needs of astronautical radio as did Andrew G. Haley.

I. Historian of Astronautical Rocketry

Another of Haley's contributions to astronautical literature was his assembly and publication of an illustrated history of the international progress in rocketry prior to and during the 20th century. Haley's *Rocketry and Space Exploration* was published in 1958, with the sub-title *The International Story*. This work is commendable in connection with the history of rocketry, but it is also one of the very few sources in English in which one can find details about the emergence of non-governmental astronautical organizations around the world following the Second World War. Haley felt a continual compulsion to inform all potentially interested persons about the organizational developments related to rocketry at home in the US and abroad. During the 1960s Haley took substantial satisfaction from noting his works addressing issues of space law were being translated and published in other languages for foreign audiences.[33]

32 *Id.* at 3.

33 As examples: A. G. Haley, *Droit de l'espace et metadroit (Limites de jurisdiction), Revue Générale de l'Air* 1957, p.1]; AGH, *Weltraumrecht und Recht ausserhalb der Erde, Abgrenzung der Rechtsgebiete, Weltraumfahrt*, 1957, *Heft* 2, S. 57, *Heft* 3, S. 69; AGH, Derecho

In addition to his published works, there are manuscripts of at least two books drafted by Haley, but never published. These manuscripts are in the retained files of Andrew Haley held in part by the National Air and Space Museum of the Smithsonian Institution, and at the Archives on Space Law maintained by the National Center for Remote Sensing, Air and Space Law at the University of Mississippi. The unpublished manuscripts at Mississippi include *The First Book of Space Law*, the introduction and chapters V through XII. It is assumed that this project was stopped, but not abandoned, at about 1958, when Haley learned through research that there had already been books published on space law. The second unpublished manuscript is *All the World's Rockets*, introduction and chapters 1 through 7. This project was pursued, revised, expanded, retitled and appeared as the book *Rocketry and Space Exploration* in 1958. (Van Nostrand Co., New York, 1958, 334 pp.[34]

Although Haley concluded that he would not publish the first book on space law, he was determined to collect and digest all that he could of the burgeoning body of space law and to publish a book about the law. In 1960, he engaged a recent Harvard Law School graduate, Robert D. Crane, to compile all of Haley's works on space law in a bound collection of several volumes. In 1962, upon Crane's recommendation, Haley hired the then rising third year law student at Duke Law School, Stephen Doyle, to extract from the papers, collected chronologically by Crane, a topical integration and general commentary on space law. A first manuscript of the intended resulting book was delivered to Haley in September 1962, allowing him to edit, expand and correct the manuscript before delivering it to the Meredith Publishing Company to consider for publication, early in 1963. The book was published as *Space Law and Government*, Appleton Century Crofts, New York, 1963, 584 pp.

As summarily recounted above, Haley applied a great deal of his personal energy to the development of laws related to the use of satellites. Having

interplanetario, *Ingeniera Aeronautics, Mayo-Junio* 1958, p. 7; AGH, *Les Communications spatiales de la prochaine generation, Journal de Telecommunications, Fevrier,* 1962, p. 39. In all, there were twelve such foreign articles published in six different countries.

34 *See* on line the content of the Andrew G. Haley Collection, Law School Archives, University of Mississippi Grisham Law Library, The University of Mississippi, http://www.spacelaw.olemiss.edu/archives/haley/ last visited July 5, 2012.

substantial duplicating machinery, financial resources, and available staff, in the summer of 1966 Haley self-published a book, with printed hard covers and bound with an Acco fastener, entitled *Satellite Communications*. The content of the book comprises articles, historical surveys, and papers Haley had produced since 1955. This was only a few months before his death in October 1966. Haley clearly wanted to collect and compile all that he had done on satellite communication law between two covers and he decided to do it himself and have it done.[35] At the same time that he was compiling the book *Satellite Communications*, Haley published a comprehensive and detailed account of the roles of the American Rocket Society and the International Astronautical Federation in the regulatory activities related to satellite communications.[36]

In addition to his work for the IAF and the ARS on astronautical radio needs, participating in a successful private law partnership, and assembling over several years the manuscripts of published and unpublished books, Haley continually published papers and articles dealing with selected elements and broad concepts of space law from the mid 1950s until his death in 1966. A relatively complete bibliography of his works can be seen at the end of *Space Law and Government* at pages 529 through 539, totaling about 250 separate works, and not including works published after early 1963.

J. Initiator, Commentator on and Recorder of Space Law

Andrew Haley had many fixed ideas about what was needed and what should be done about space law. In many of his early articles Haley featured reference to the 15th century Spanish jurists Francisco de Vitoria and Francisco Suarez who wrote extensively about the reliance on "Natural Law" as an appropriate basis of international law. Haley referred to later works of Hugo Grotius as an extension and application of the Spanish philosophies.[37] But

35 A. G. Haley, *Satellite Communications*, Haley, Bader and Potts, Wash., D. C., unpaginated, 1966.

36 A. G. Haley, "Space Age Radio-Frequency Allocations", *Astronautics & Aeronautics*, May 1966.

37 *See* A. G. Haley, "Space Law and Metalaw – A Synoptic View", *Harvard Law Record*, Nov. 8, 1956; and "Recent Developments in Space Law and Metalaw", vol. 24, no. 2, Harvard Law Record, Feb. 7, 1957.

Haley contended that the structure of international law in the twentieth century, being based on the laws of nations and the commonalities found therein, was inadequate to consider as a basis of law for future relationships with communities established or discovered beyond the Earth.

Haley proposed a new concept of law which he referred to as Metalaw, to be applicable to man in social constructs beyond the Earth. For reasons he took pains to elaborate, he concluded that the primary maxim or first precept of Metalaw must be "Do unto others as they would have you do unto them."[38]

A second frequent feature of Haley's writings during the latter half of the 1950s was emphasis on the importance of placing an upper limit on national sovereignty. With John Cobb Cooper, Oscar Schachter, C. Wilfred Jenks and other commentators, Haley believed it was imperative that the international community should decide early upon an agreed upper limit on national sovereignty. Haley championed the view that the "primary jurisdictional line" between air space and outer space should be based on Theodore von Kármán's observations concerning the terminal altitude of aerodynamic lift, allowing an aircraft to "fly" in airspace. Von Kármán observed that as aircraft ascended to higher altitudes the density of the air decreases until a point is reached where an aircraft could not lift itself higher above the earth. As Haley explained: "...in the corridor of continuous flight when an object reaches approximately 275,000 feet and is travelling at 35,000 feet per second, the Kepler [centrifugal] force takes over and the aerodynamic lift is gone. This is the critical jurisdictional boundary."[39] Thus Haley latterly proposed and promoted an upper limit of national sovereignty at approximately 52 miles.

Perhaps Haley's most elaborate and fully documented arguments concerning the appropriate nature of space law are contained in his seminal paper on "Basic Concepts of Space Law," presented at the 25th Annual Meeting of the American Rocket Society in Chicago, Illinois in November 1955.[40] In this

38 A. G. Haley, *Space Law and Government*, Ch. 12, 394-423, and sources cited there.

39 A. G. Haley, "Space Law and Metalaw – Jurisdiction Defined", 24:3 *Journal of Air Law & Commerce* 286, 297, summer 1957.

40 A. G. Haley, "Basic Concepts of Space Law – The Unmanned Earth Satellite", a paper presented to the 25th Annual Meeting of the American Rocket Society in Chicago, ARS Reprint 277-55, Nov. 14-18, 1955; published as "Basic Concepts of Space Law", 26 *Jet Propulsion* 951-957, Nov. 1956.

1955 paper Haley addressed the extent of the known universe and the likelihood of other sentient societies existing on other worlds. This was his rationale for consideration of the need for Metalaw. He then offered a background discussion of the recognition of absolute national jurisdiction in superjacent airspace, which required a determination of an upper limit of national sovereignty. Haley argued that the United Nations should establish a commission "to study the legal and jurisdictional questions and an effort should be made to reach an understanding among all nations on these [jurisdictional] questions."[41] In the next section of his paper Haley addressed the rapidly emerging need for communications laws and controls, particularly the need for allocation of sufficient radiomagnetic spectrum to facilitate spaceflight and operations of spacecraft with radio controls. In this connection Haley was personally convinced that the necessary international regulatory machinery to obtain necessary decisions existed, it remained only for nations to realize the need for early action.

During 1956 Haley further developed his positions on a wider variety of topics within his view of the necessary scope of space law. In an extensive paper, published in the *Harvard Law Record* in November 1956, Haley added discussion of the adequacies and inadequacies of existing international law, questions related to traveling in space, and the needs for an administrative licensing authority, and the emerging questions related to exploration of space.[42]

During the 1950s Haley became more and more involved in the affairs of the International Astronautical Federation. He aggressively represented and promoted the international interests of the Federation, particularly seeking status to participate in meetings of organizations including the International Council of Scientific Unions (ICSU), the United Nations Educational, Scientific and Cultural Organization (UNESCO), and the International Telecommunication Union (ITU). In his work with the Federation he came in contact with many of the pioneering jurists of the period and communicated with them frequently. Correspondence survives indicating contact with John

41 A. G. Haley, "Basic Concepts of Space Law", 26 *Jet Propulsion* 957, Nov. 1956.

42 A. G. Haley, "Space Law and Metalaw – A Synoptic View", *Harvard Law Record*, Nov. 8, 1956; and "Recent Developments in Space Law and Metalaw", vol. 24, no. 2, *Harvard Law Record*, Feb. 7, 1957.

Cobb Cooper, first Director of the McGill Institute of Air and Space Law in Montreal; Alex Meyer, Director of the Institute on Air and Space Law at the University of Cologne; Leonid Sedov and Vladlen Vereshchetin of the USSR Academy of Sciences, Vladimir Kopal in Czechoslovakia, and many others.[43]

Limitations of space in this essay preclude an elaboration of all the issues, arguments and publications concerning space law, introduced and promoted by Andrew G. Haley. An excellent survey of his major works and ideas is contained in his 1963 book *Space Law and Government.* A well-researched and documented history of Haley's life is in Shirley Thomas' biographical collection, *Men of Space,* volume 7 at pp. 138-159.

The Haley papers collections at the University of Mississippi and at the National Air and Space Museum in Washington, D. C., contain many detailed historical records, including copies of correspondence with industrial and governmental leaders in many nations. Because of his expressed interest in the establishment and development of national organizations involved in rocketry and astronautics Haley received and often published news about the emerging organizations in many countries, which is especially notable in his 1958 book on *Rocketry and Space Exploration.*[44]

K. Philanthropist

During his working years of the 1950s and the 1960s Haley regularly applied his financial resources to the betterment or improved condition of others. In 1953 he established by endowment the American Rocket Society Astronautics Award, which continues to be administered today by the American Institute of Aeronautics and Astronautics. In 1960 he also established and funded the A. G. Haley Gold Medal Award of the International Institute of Space Law, to recognize excellence in contributions to the development of international space law. Haley regularly supported students who wished to travel to and participate in meetings and conferences on space law, and frequently had

43 *See* on line the content of the Andrew G. Haley Collection, Law School Archives, University of Mississippi Grisham Law Library, http://www.spacelaw.olemiss.edu/archives/haley/, last visited July 5, 2012.

44 A. G. Haley, *Rocketry and Space Exploration, op. cit. supra*, note 10, at Chapter 13, The working Societies, 269-291.

two or more local law students employed as summer interns in his law firm in Washington, which was both a financial boon and an extraordinary learning experience for those lucky enough to enjoy this largess.

L. Conclusion

Andrew G. Haley was a complicated man of many parts. He was an attorney widely recognized for excellence in the communications field. He was an industrial leader and stimulator of interest in rocketry and astronautics. He was a world-wide traveler and accomplished author of many works, published and unpublished. He was without doubt an early and articulate proponent of space law and he enjoyed an undeniable place of leadership and accomplishment in early development of international space law and related organizations.

Haley's extraordinary life ended at Georgetown University Hospital on Saturday, September 10, 1966, just over two months prior to his 62nd birthday. His death occasioned an extraordinary outpouring of compassion for his family and remorse for loss of his presence from this life. The American Institute of Aeronautics and Astronautics, published a well illustrated obituary in their monthly magazine. The Institute received permission from Haley's family to select some of the world-wide expressions of condolences and regrets and to publish them in conjunction with the obituary.[45]

As a man of many interests and pursuits, there were and are few men like him who work as hard, who care as much about the need for order in our world community, and who are willing to devote their lives and substantial portions of their fortunes to the welfare of the commwealth. Andrew Gallagher Haley was an important figure in early astronautical history as well as in the history of space law.

45 *See* Stephen E. Doyle, "Astronautics Loses an Original: Andrew G. Haley", *Astronautics and Aeronautics*, Nov. 1966, 60-65, *see* especially the telegraphic messages at 64-65.

A Selected Bibliography[46]

Books

Haley, A. G., *Rocketry and Space Exploration*, D. van Nostrand Co., Princeton, 1958, 334 pp. with index.

Haley, A. G., *Space Law and Government*, Appleton-Century-Crofts, New York, 1963, 584 pp. with index.

Selected Articles and Papers (from a total of more than 200 works)

Haley, A. G., "Basic Concepts of Space Law – The Unmanned Earth Satellite", a paper presented to the 25th Annual Meeting of the American Rocket Society in Chicago, ARS Reprint 277-55, Nov. 14-18, 1955; published as "Basic Concepts of Space Law", 26 *Jet Propulsion* 951-957, Nov. 1956.

__________, "Space Law and Metalaw – A Synoptic View," paper presented to the VIIth Annual Congress of the International Astronautical Federation, Rome, Italy, September, 1956, published in *Proceedings of the VIIth International Astronautical Congress*, Associazione Italiana Razzi, Rome, Italy, 1956. Also published in *Zeitschrift für Luftrecht*, University of Cologne, Germany. Later referred to by Haley as the "First Essay on Metalaw."

__________, "Recent Developments in Space Law and Metalaw," paper presented to the 11th Annual meeting of the American Rocket Society, New York, New York, November 1956, published in 24:2 *Harvard Law Record*, Cambridge, Mass., Feb., 1957. Later referred to by Haley as the "Second Essay on Metalaw."

46 For copies of many articles, papers and unpublished drafts of books by Haley, *see* on line the content of the Andrew G. Haley Collection, Law School Archives, University of Mississippi, Grisham Law Library, http://www.spacelaw.olemiss.edu/archives/haley/ (last visited July 5, 2012).

__________, "Space Law and Metalaw – Jurisdiction Defined", 24:3 *Journal of Air Law & Commerce,* summer 1957; also published in 16:8 *J. B. I. S.,* July-Aug. 1958, 472-482.

__________, "Space Age Presents Immediate Legal Problems," paper presented to the First Colloquium on the Law of Outer Space, The Hague, Aug. 1958, in the *Proceedings of the First Colloquium on the Law of Outer Space,* originally published by Springer-Verlag, Vienna, 1959, reprinted by permission in 1997 by the International Institute of Space Law, Paris, pp. 5-27.

__________, "The International Astronautical Federation and Space Communications", Remarks before the Delegates to the Administrative Radio Conference of the ITU, Geneva, Oct., 1959.

__________, "Space Exploration – the Problems of Today, Tomorrow and in the Future," paper presented to the Second Colloquium on the Law of Outer Space, London, 1959, in the *Proceedings of the Second Colloquium on the Law of Outer Space,* originally published by Springer-Verlag, Vienna, 1960, reprinted by permission in 1997 by the International Institute of Space Law, Paris, pp. 44-58.

__________,"Survey of Legal Opinion on Extraterrestrial Jurisdiction," paper presented to the Third Colloquium on the Law of Outer Space, Stockholm, 1960, in the *Proceedings of the Third Colloquium on the Law of Outer Space,* originally published by AB ÅETÅ-TRYCK, Åhlén & Åkerlunds Tryckerier, Stockholm, 1961, reprinted by permission in 1997 by the International Institute of Space Law, Paris, pp. 37-92.

__________, "Metalaw – The Science of Universal Jurisprudence, the Third Essay," paper presented to the Fourth Colloquium on the Law of Outer Space, Washington, D. C., 1961, in the *Proceedings of the Fourth Colloquium on the Law of Outer Space,* published by the University of Oklahoma Research Institute, Norman, OK, 1963, pp. 27-57

__________, "Space Communications – Some Legal and Sociological Aspects," paper presented to the Fifth Colloquium on the Law of Outer Space, Varna, Bulgaria, September 1962, published by A. G. Haley for the IISL, Washington, D. C., 1963, unpaginated.

__________, "Medical Jurisprudence in Outer Space," paper presented to the Sixth Colloquium on the Law of Outer Space, Paris, France, September 1963, published by A. G. Haley for the IISL, Washington, D. C., 1964, unpaginated.

__________, "Space Age Radio Frequency Allocation", *Astronautics &Aeronautics*, May 1966.

Works about Andrew G. Haley

Broadcasting, Washington, D. C. magazine, "Our Respects to Andrew Gallagher Haley", Nov. 11, 1957, Washington, D. C.

Thomas, Shirley, *Men of Space*, Volume 7, at 136-159, Chilton Books, Philadelphia, 1965.

Doyle, S. E., "Astronautics Loses an Original: Andrew G. Haley", *Astronautics and Aeronautics*, Nov. 1966, monthly magazine of the American Institute of Aeronautics and Astronautics, pp. 60-65.

Doyle, S. E., "Andrew Gallagher Haley: A Biographical Sketch (1904-1996)," published in *The Eagle has Returned, the Second Part, Proceedings of the Dedication Conference of the International Space Hall of Fame*, Alamogordo, New Mexico, October 1976; Volume 45, Science and Technology Series, American Astronautical Society, 1977, copyright held by the New Mexico Research Institute.

Haley, Christopher T., *Great Grandfather Tells All*, a self-published personal memoir produced for Haley family members, 1981, see particularly pp. 39-48.

Chapter VII **Daniel Goedhuis** (31.1.1905 – 5.10.1995)

Peter van Fenema* and Tanja Masson-Zwaan**

A. Introduction – The Period up to World War II

> Looking back on my life, the first thing I realize is how very lucky I have been and how grateful I should be that fate or chance gave me the opportunity to participate in some ways in the revolutionary changes which resulted from the conquest of air and outer space.

Professor Daniel ("Daan") Goedhuis wrote these words in 1994 in a manuscript called "[s]ome recollections of an international life", in which he recorded his memories of, in particular, his war-time experiences. He was about 89 years old and lived in England, where, when not travelling abroad, he would reside most of his life.

That he had indeed lived an international life becomes clear when one considers his curriculum vitae, which shows his fascination with two fields of law, air law and space law, both of which made him travel all over the world.[1]

* Adjunct professor of law, McGill University, Institute of Air and Space Law, Montreal, Canada.

** Assistant professor/Deputy Director, International Institute of Air and Space Law, Leiden University, Leiden, The Netherlands.

1 Goedhuis' background and experience in the field of air law and of – bilateral and multilateral – aviation negotiations deserve attention because they shaped him (and v.v.) and were of decisive influence on his approach, right from the start and up to the end, to the development of space law.

Stephan Hobe (ed.), Pioneers of Space Law
© 2013 *International Institute of Space Law.* ISBN *978-90-04-24027-8. pp. 99-125*

It all started in 1922 when, invited by English friends to come and stay with them in London, the adventurous 17-year old convinced his father that it would benefit his education to *fly* to his destination. In fact, the first flight of Dutch airline KLM, founded in 1919, had taken place less than one year thereafter from Croydon Airport in London to Amsterdam, and in 1921 scheduled services between the two cities had started, operated with Fokker aircraft.

It was not so much the 4-hours flight from Amsterdam via Calais to Dover and onward to London that impressed him as the treatment after arrival: through the excitement of flying for the first time he had forgotten his passport. Thus expecting trouble upon arrival, he was greatly relieved when the KLM representative, a former captain of the British army who had been interned in Holland during the first World War, considered the lack of the document completely irrelevant, took a piece of paper on which he put a stamp of KLM and told Goedhuis that that was his passport.

With that experience with (the power of) the air company, it is not surprising that less than seven years later, after having obtained his law degree at Leiden University – with a one-year interruption to join the Dutch cavalry and be appointed Second Lieutenant – he joined KLM as legal advisor, reporting in that position to the Corporate Secretary and to the formidable founder and President of KLM, "Flying Dutchman" Albert Plesman.

He did not stay long in that position at KLM's head office in The Hague: in 1931 he was offered the function of head of the Central Office of the International Air Traffic Association (IATA), an association already created in 1919 by the representatives of six European air companies, mostly *in statu nascendi.*

The Central Office, under the Secretary-General, managed IATA, and Goedhuis had to deal with economic, political and strategic aspects of international aviation relations. But he soon concentrated on an important legal aspect of international air transport, the liability of air carriers in case of accidents and delay. In 1929, a Diplomatic Conference in Warsaw had produced an international convention addressing these issues. However, the application and interpretation of this Convention in practice had led to considerable conflict, and Goedhuis decided to write a treatise on that topic in the form of a doctoral thesis to be submitted to Leiden University.

In 1933, Goedhuis successfully defended this dissertation, written in the French language and entitled *"La Convention de Varsovie"*, and was accorded the title of Doctor of Law. The published version of the thesis, for quite some time being the only treatise on (the interpretation of) the Warsaw Convention, apparently became a bestseller.

In the following years Goedhuis continued to study this topic of private air law, and even published another acclaimed book on the matter in 1937 called "National Air Legislations and the Warsaw Convention."

But slowly, both through his work for IATA and for KLM, his focus shifted to public air law, to the aviation relations between states governed by the "Convention relating to the Regulations of Aerial Navigation", adopted at the Peace Conference in Versailles in 1919. Put differently, Goedhuis started to address the struggle between the international aspirations of state airlines on the one hand and the principle of state sovereignty over national air space enshrined in the above Convention on the other hand.

On the latter issue he published his first article in the *Revue de Droit International et de Législation Comparée* of 1936; it was entitled *"Le régime juridique de l'Espace Aérien".*

His work for IATA included the organization of the two-yearly conferences of the Association held in different European cities. In his "Recollections" he recalls a number of events related to these conferences that left an indelible impression.

One experience as early as 1931 involved his post-Conference travel from Budapest to Amsterdam. Being told by the KLM representative in Budapest that a KLM plane returning from Indonesia (then the Dutch Indies) would make a stop in Budapest, Goedhuis decided to cancel his train reservation and opt for the KLM flight to Amsterdam. That same day he was informed that the train had been blown up by a bomb placed by a "madman", killing several people amongst whom, as he saw for himself at the place of the accident, the president of Sabena and his wife with whom he was supposed to have travelled. "Fate" indeed!

The KLM plane did not wait for him, so it was several days later that Goedhuis arrived by train in Holland and heard that head office was far from pleased about the lack of communication about his (non-) involvement in the train accident. In fact, when he visited his boss at home to explain things he was met at the door by the six-year old son of Plesman who exclaimed: "how furious daddy will be when he sees that you are still alive!"

In the pre-war period, IATA convened every year in Berlin a Traffic Conference hosted by the Directors of Lufthansa. The one in 1938 was particularly eventful for a number of reasons. It involved a huge party in the *Staatsoper* (State Opera House) to celebrate the birthday of Field Marshall Goering (who, behind the façade of Lufthansa was building up the military air force), in the presence of the leading officials of the Nazi party and of the top of the military establishment. The next day, after a lively lunch with Goering, (apparently "an excellent and amusing host"), Rudolf Hess, Hitler's deputy, took the chairman of the Conference, a Norwegian general who headed Norwegian Airlines, and Goedhuis to meet Adolf Hitler. After introductions, Hitler delivered a speech in which he explained how international aviation would enhance peace in the world, in retrospect an interesting statement with war preparations already well on their way! In his "Recollections", Goedhuis remarks that, after Hitler has talked with him personally about the possible role of international aviation in improving international relations: "I received some understanding of how Hitler was able to influence to such an extraordinary extent so many of his compatriots."

B. World War II

In August 1939, the Dutch government mobilized the army and reserve Cavalry officer Goedhuis was called to duty. He was attached to a regiment equipped with horses (for primarily ceremonial purposes) and, until the German army invaded Holland in May 1940 and the Regiment was provided with armored cars, he spent most of his time at the barracks giving riding instructions to the soldiers under his command (Goedhuis had learnt to ride at Cavalry school in 1923, participated in and won competitions, and, as he put it himself in his Recollections, "was very lucky that my legal and diplomatic work did not prevent me from indulging in my love of horses and equestrianism"). The Dutch army soon capitulated and Goedhuis, after a brief imprisonment by the Germans ended through the intermediary of a Lufthansa colleague, went into hiding, a situation which lasted almost two years. In that period, he used his ample free time to write an article, "Civil Aviation after the War", which was smuggled out of Holland and was published in 1942 in the American Journal of International Law. He also wrote his "Handbook on Air Law" which came out in 1943 but was immediately confiscated by the

German Occupation Authority. Fortunately, Nijhoff Publishers managed to get back the copies distributed to the various bookshops and was able to store these until the end of the war: the book came on the market (again) in 1945. Goedhuis had been able to secretly send one copy of the book to Professor Telders, his friend and colleague of Leiden University, who had been deported to the Buchenwald concentration camp. Telders, after his transfer to Camp Bergen Belsen, obtained information from Russian prisoners about a secret communist network in Holland, and used the book to record this information in code. When Telders died in Bergen Belsen the book disappeared, and all efforts by the Dutch Ministry of Foreign Affairs to trace it failed.

This is not the place to recall Goedhuis' experiences during the war, interesting and revealing as they may be. Suffice to say that in the course of 1943 Plesman made it known that Goedhuis was needed in London to keep an eye on KLM's British branch and the latter was quite prepared to comply with this request. After a number of attempts, he succeeded to escape occupied Holland in January 1944 and, after a lengthy and dangerous overland voyage through Belgium, France and Spain ended up in Gibraltar from where he flew, via Rabat, to London, where he would stay and work until the end of the war. His wife, whom he had married in 1939, remained in occupied Holland all that time.

Interesting from the point of view of his professional life is his work in the field of aviation in London. With the IATA office in The Hague seen as German controlled, the British, Dutch, French, Belgian, Norwegian and Polish allied representatives had decided to establish a temporary IATA office in London. Goedhuis was asked to join in the capacity of Secretary-General, the same function he had performed in The Hague.

At one of these meetings it was decided that the most important aim of IATA after the war was the inclusion of all the important airlines in the world as members. For that purpose, in 1944 Goedhuis was sent to Chicago with the task to convince all US airlines, organized in the American Air Transport Organization, to join the Association. This mission proved successful and the parties concerned decided to convene a conference at which all leading airlines of the world would be invited, to set up a new IATA.

C. After World War II – Goedhuis as International Aviation Negotiator

This Conference took place in 1945 in Havana, and a new IATA was created with Headquarters in Montreal. Goedhuis was asked for the post of Secretary General of IATA but decided not to accept this function. He had two good reasons for that decision. First, already in 1938 Goedhuis had been appointed lecturer in air law at Leiden University and he wanted to continue his academic work there. Secondly, the Minister of Foreign Affairs had asked him already before the Havana Conference to join the Dutch Diplomatic Service. The idea was that Goedhuis, as a diplomat, would be charged with negotiations with– at first – primarily European countries to obtain landing rights, that is market access, for KLM. In December 1945 he was thus appointed Civil Air Attaché with the rank of Counselor, at the Netherlands Embassy in London. London was vital for Dutch and KLM aviation interests in view of the vital air connections with the Dutch Indies and the related need for transit/landing rights in India and other territories under British control. A year later he was appointed in the same function at the Embassies in Paris, Brussels, Madrid, Lisbon and the Scandinavian countries: being on the diplomatic list of these countries was seen as helpful in the negotiations. The administrative burden connected with the proper execution of these diplomatic functions led to the decision to later limit these to London, Paris, Madrid and Lisbon.

Given KLM's appetite for worldwide landing rights, Goedhuis had to lead a substantial number of missions to some 30 countries. None of these were a walkover, virtually all took days and sometimes weeks, and a lot of lobbying, to yield results. In virtually all cases this was caused by the national state airlines concerned who feared competition from KLM and had little interest themselves in opening services between their country and Holland. The Chicago Convention of 1944 which regulated post-war international civil aviation of all allied countries and their friends had *not* produced a system of free competition amongst all international airlines as proposed by the U.S. with the support of the Netherlands and the Scandinavian countries. In stead, the majority of the participants had followed the U.K. philosophy of strict national controls of access by foreign airlines, which resulted in articles 1 and 6 of the Convention respectively confirming the complete and exclusive sovereignty of states over their national air space and forbidding foreign aircraft to operate scheduled services into those states without explicit prior approval of the state concerned. The rule thus became: if an airline wants to start services to a foreign country, the airline's national government has to negotiate a treaty with the foreign government concerned to make those services possible. Overall diplomatic relations, politics and ad hoc alliances would further complicate matters and would turn simple requests for market access into "cloak and dagger" type of maneuvers and even clandestine and illegal nightly operations through foreign air space[2].

In view of the U.S. "free competition" stand during the Chicago Conference, the Netherlands negotiating team led by Goedhuis in 1946 was confident that Washington would give ample rights for KLM to exploit the U.S. market. However, some days before the delegation arrived, the U.S. Senate, no doubt inspired by the respective U.S. airlines, had abandoned the liberal aviation policy of 1944. As a result, after difficult and frustrating negotiations the disappointed delegation had to content itself with permission for air services to New York only.

Bilateral aviation negotiations with other countries followed, Australia, Brazil (where, on board of a small military aircraft, he survived a crash in the jungle), Argentina, Japan, but also European countries such as the U.K. (which was far from eager to give KLM permission to fly to British colonies in the East), Belgium, Spain and Italy.

In the latter country, Goedhuis had the unusual experience to have his former boss and president of KLM, Plesman, in the delegation. Plesman had invited himself and, as it turned out, for a reason that had little to do with KLM landing rights to Italy. Goedhuis as chairman of the delegation was understandably afraid that this very forceful personality would try to dominate the talks, but Plesman behaved. When the talks had led to a satisfactory arrangement on KLM's services to and through Rome, the Dutch ambassador accompanied Goedhuis and Plesman to the Vatican for the audience that the ambassador had arranged with Pope Pius XII. Plesman had a large envelope in his hands and, responding to Goedhuis' question, said that it contained his "peace plan" which he wanted to discuss with the Pope. With this "rather crankish" plan (as Goedhuis called it), Plesman tried to use his outstanding

2 *See* Marc Dierikx, *Daniel Goedhuis – Diplomat in Air Law*, 4 Journaal Luchtrecht 13-18, at 17 (2009).

reputation in the field of international aviation cooperation to convince political leaders to help him create political and peaceful relationships in the world. The Dutch Foreign Office, afraid of this plan being seen as a government sponsored project, tried several times but in vain to make him abandon his intention to discuss this plan with foreign governments: Plesman had simply ignored these efforts to curtail his missionary endeavors.

Goedhuis' Recollections should be quoted in full here:

> Plesman having asked me whether I would mind if he would talk first to the Pope, started, after we had been introduced, with a lengthy explanation of his peace plan and said that, as the Pope was the religious leader of more than 600 million people in the world, his support of this plan would have a momentous influence on the enhancement of international peaceful relations between states. The Pope, obviously becoming impatient with Plesman's verbosity, tried, by raising his hand, to stop Plesman's flux de parole, but did not have any success. When the Pope had finally said that he would study the plan, Plesman ended his discourse, and after having talked to me for about five minutes, the Pope gave us his blessing. As to what happened with the peace plan, it was not difficult to foresee that oblivion was its ultimate fate.

In the late 1950s, Goedhuis was increasingly confronted with new and younger Dutch negotiators flexing their muscles, both in the Civil Aviation Department and at KLM, the latter in particular in the person of one of his former students and *promovendi* Dr. Henri ("Or") Wassenbergh – who had been working for KLM since 1950 and would later also succeed him as Professor at Leiden University.

In January 1961, his function was officially terminated, and the Minister of Foreign Affairs showed his appreciation for all the negotiating work done by appointing him "Honorary Consultant for civil aviation issues." Goedhuis stayed in London, but would continue to frequently travel to Leiden University for the purpose of lecturing on air and space law.

D. Goedhuis as Academic and Author

In 1938 Goedhuis, apart from being appointed Secretary General of IATA, also got his appointment as lecturer in air law at Leiden University. In the same year, when the International Law Association held its 40th Conference in The Hague, he joined the Dutch Branch of that Association and became member of its Air Law Committee. After the war, in 1947, he was appointed professor of air law[3], also at Leiden University.

In the field of air law he wrote a solid number of articles. There were basically two general topics he concentrated on: private air law, i.e. the Warsaw Convention, the topic of his doctoral thesis and subsequent book on that liability instrument, and public air law, which in particular after the war reflected his work as a government representative in bilateral aviation negotiations. As observed before, the latter task boiled down to fighting for free market access for the national airline with nations that relied on the principle of sovereignty over national air space to deny such access in the interest of their own airline. Thus, finding legal, political and practical arguments to limit the application of that principle for the benefit of international (commercial) relations became an important theme in his publications.

As for the Warsaw Convention, problems of interpretation and application, including unhappiness with the low ceiling of liability of the air carriers towards passengers and shippers, led to a Diplomatic Conference in 1955 to amend the Convention. The Hague was chosen as the venue ("in the shadow of the Peace Palace"), and Goedhuis, in view of his influential publications on this issue, was elected chairman.

The result of the Conference, the Hague Protocol, was welcomed by the world of aviation as a much-needed modernization of an old treaty, and Goedhuis was warmly praised for a job well done:

> He has known how to carry out the work of this Conference with smiling firmness. He has overcome difficulties because he knows that sometimes it is better not to solve them immediately... he directed [the debate] to a successful outcome and with a sense of timeliness in regard to the development of the discussion for which he should have our warm thanks.

3 *See* Idea and Interest in International Aviation, Inaugural Address delivered by Goedhuis on the occasion of his appointment as Professor of Air Law at Leiden University (1947).

With that task accomplished, Goedhuis effectively left the field of the development of private air law to others.

For a few more years, public air law remained important *inter alia* because of his work as a government aviation negotiator. His lectures at Leiden University, for which he would fly to Holland every two weeks, of course dealt with both private and public air law and amply showed his knowledge and experience in both fields. In 1954 he gave a course at the *Académie de Droit International de La Haye* in the Peace Palace in The Hague, "Questions of Public International Air Law", in which the topics air sovereignty and bilateral aviation relations featured prominently. And in his article in the Netherlands International Law Review of 1955, entitled "The concept of sovereignty in air law", he described sovereignty over national air space as a problem that seriously hampered the growth of international aviation in general and – of course – of Dutch aviation in particular.

E. Goedhuis and Space Law

> When in the middle of the 1950s it became ever clearer that the effort both by the U.S. and by the Soviet Union to develop human activities in outer space might soon have results, I decided to concentrate my studies primarily on the legal, political, military and economic problems with which the world community would be faced in this new era. It was in particular my membership of the "International Law Association" which enabled me to take some part in the creation of rules to govern space activities.

In his "Recollections", from which this text is quoted, Goedhuis makes clear that the ILA, of which he had been a member since 1938, was his preferred forum for discussing the future rules of space law. The ILA had dealt with questions of air law since its 27th Conference in Paris in 1912, with as first topics aerial collisions, air sovereignty and the freedom of air space (!). It had eminent air law specialists in its Air Law Committee, who, after some initial hesitation, proved eager to broaden their horizon and focus on outer space.

In 1956, at the 47th Conference in Dubrovnik, the Air Law Committee convened. Illustrious members such as Beaumont, Garnault, Chauvau, Smirnoff, Berezowski and Pépin discussed, among a number of other issues, also Daniel Goedhuis' Report, entitled "The limitation of Air Sovereignty". In that report, the author traced the results of a number of Conferences starting with the International Conference on Air Navigation in Paris of 1910 up to the ICAO Conference in Geneva of 1947 "to develop a multilateral agreement on the exchange of commercial rights in international civil air transport", and analyzed the views and attitudes of states with respect to the concept of air sovereignty up to 1956. He also reviewed the work done within the ILA on this issue since 1913.

Goedhuis stayed clear from postulating that air sovereignty was *de iure* limited by freedom of passage, let alone by the freedom to land in foreign countries for commercial purposes, but maintained that through the years some states and some experts had supported the idea of innocent passage in the interest of international commerce and international communications, this in contrast to the "fetish of an ultra-sovereignty" prevalent in 1947. Goedhuis approvingly quoted a recommendation adopted by the 36th ILA Conference in New York in 1930:

> Each Contracting Party (when not a belligerent) should undertake to accord freedom of innocent passage above its territory to private aircraft of the other Contracting Parties provided that the conditions laid down by the law are applied with.

Goedhuis then proposed to adopt the following recommendations:

> *The International Law Association,*
> Considering the highly important role international aviation can play in a balanced growth of world economy resulting in raising living standards all over the world,
> Considering that through the increase of general prosperity the chances of peace are being furthered, recommends:
> I. that States which have not as yet signed the International Air Services Transit Agreement[4] do so without undue delay;

4 The multilateral International Air Services Transit Agreement, signed at Chicago in 1944, gives the airlines of the parties to the Agreement the right to fly through the air space of all the other parties and to land in the territories of those parties for technical and operational, *i.e.* non-commercial, purposes, without the need for prior approval of the States concerned. These rights are also referred to as the two "technical

II. that in questions regarding the granting of commercial landing rights to foreign operators the States let themselves be guided by the basic principle that the social and economic needs of the individual are served by having at his disposal the most extensive international air communications possible;
And that, therefore, apart from specific national interests there is a common interest in expanding those communications upon which greater emphasis than heretofore should be laid;
Furthermore, that in granting such landing rights the principle of non-discrimination which is at the basis of Chicago Convention should be strictly adhered to.

Goedhuis, with this report and this draft recommendation, clearly followed in the footsteps of Grotius, whose "*Mare Liberum*" was meant, or at least served in practice, to promote the freedom of the Dutch to navigate the seas in pursuit of their commercial interests.

In the ILA Air Law Committee, it was Pépin the scholar who called Goedhuis the negotiator to order. In an addendum to the Report, Pépin and John Cobb Cooper, then respectively Director and former Director of the Institute of International Air Law, McGill University, discussing only the question of the legal status of the right of innocent passage, submitted that neither the ILA nor the international conventions quoted by Goedhuis nor State practice had shown that innocent passage was a principle of customary international law; this exception to the principle of air sovereignty existing since 1910 and confirmed in the Treaty of 1919 therefore has to be expressly agreed upon by the States concerned (e.g. by the Transit Agreement).

Pépin, no doubt with a smile, noted that the Netherlands Government in September 1915, protesting against a flight of German Zeppelins over its territory, had said:

freedoms of the air"; they are in fact exceptions to the principle of sovereignty over national air space as laid down in Article 1 of the Chicago Convention: "The contracting States recognize that every State has complete and exclusive sovereignty over the air space above its territory." In his Report, Goedhuis observed as a "bright spot" that in the mean time 43 States, together operating nearly 90% of world air traffic with the exclusion of Soviet Union and China, had signed the Transit Agreement.

> Flying over the territory of a State without its consent is incompatible with respect to its sovereignty.

In his written reaction, Goedhuis rightly corrected the impression created by Pépin that his Report had suggested the right of passage as a rule of customary international law: Goedhuis himself had in fact called that idea "wishful thinking" of some writers. In his closing remark on the matter Goedhuis implicitly criticized the *de lege lata* approach of Pépin by referring to the Constitution of the ILA, observing:

> [...] the members should concern themselves, not only with descriptions of how States behave, but with prescriptions for how States *ought* to behave in the interest of the international community.

When Goedhuis introduced his Report in the meeting, he unexpectedly (?) added a proposed recommendation to the above two mentioned in his Report. It read as follows:

> that the Air Law Committee continues the study of the nature and contents of air sovereignty, paying special attention to the problems connected with coming flights in outer space. (*emph. add.*)

After an interesting and lively discussion, all three recommendations proposed by Goedhuis were adopted, proving both a success for Goedhuis, the aviation negotiator, and marking the start of a new career as a promoter of space law. It is the latter role in which he excelled in the ILA in the many years to come.

It would not be correct to suggest that Goedhuis was the first to recognize the importance of this new field of law: Scholars like Mandl (1932!), Alex Meyer (1952: "Legal problems of space flight") and Welf Heinrich Prince of Hanover (1953: a doctoral dissertation on *"Luftrecht und Weltraum"* – Air Law and Space), but also Cooper (1951) and Schachter, Director Legal Affairs of the U.N. (1952), had preceded him with their publications on space related legal issues.[5] And

5 See for an overview of the history of space law making, S.E. Doyle, Origins of international space law and the International Institute of Space Law of the International Astronautical Federation (2002).

Andrew Haley, general counsel of the American Rocket Society, wrote at least three articles on space law in 1956, as did Wilfred Jenks and Eugène Pépin.

But it can not be denied that Goedhuis, whether, as an air law specialist, he was aware of these predecessors' work or not, took the initiative in the ILA Air Law Committee in 1956 to put space law on the agenda, and that may have influenced colleagues in other *fora*. Later in the same year the International Astronautical Federation (IAF) had its Conference in Rome, and legal aspects of space flight were discussed at that occasion. A year later, at the Barcelona Conference of the IAF, Andrew Haley presented his views on space law, followed in 1958, under Haley's presidency of the IAF, by the first Colloquium on the Law of Outer Space in The Hague. It was at that Colloquium that Pépin proposed to establish within the IAF a permanent Legal Committee to study matters of space law.

Goedhuis did not pay much attention to the IAF – later IISL – Colloquia: in the early years he appeared twice to give his views and then, concentrating on his work in the ILA, left this forum entirely to his compatriot (and competitor?) Dr. Isabella de Rode (later Diederiks) – Verschoor, at the time lecturer in air law at Utrecht University in the Netherlands. When in 1959 in London, on the proposal of Pépin, 11 (!) Working Groups were established within IAF to address virtually all imaginable space-related legal issues, most of his ILA colleagues joined, but Goedhuis stayed out: even of the W.G. on the limit of national sovereignty, the delimitation of air space/outer space and rights of passage etc., topics very close to his heart.

He did however present a brief note at the 1959 Colloquium, appropriately entitled "The question of freedom of innocent passage of space vehicles of one state through the space above the territory of another state which is not outer space", in which he observed that freedom of outer space becomes practically illusory if States do not declare themselves prepared to limit their rights *over the space above their territories which cannot be considered "outer space"* so as to allow freedom of passage for peaceful purposes. Goedhuis avoided the use of the term "air space" for definitional reasons, but basically said that if outer space is a *res communis omnium,* freedom of innocent passage through national air space is a necessary corollary.

It is interesting to note here the space lawyer Goedhuis promoting the limitation of national air sovereignty for the benefit of free space activities, where the *air lawyer* had always argued the same principle for the benefit of – as yet elusive – free airline services.

Coming back to his space law recommendation at the 1956 ILA Conference, the discussion that followed in the Air Law Committee included the Director of ICAO's Legal Bureau, Mr. Roy, who announced that the Assembly of his Organization one month earlier had adopted a resolution recognizing the growing interest amongst jurists in the legal problems relating to outer space and had noted that, although not of immediate interest, these matters would appropriately fall within the competence of that Organization.

Almost 50 years later, the President of the Council of ICAO, Dr. Kotaite, referring to the successful suborbital spaceflights of SpaceShip One, suggested in remarks reported in the French language Canadian press that ICAO would be the most appropriate organization to regulate the safety of such suborbital flights.[6]

After unreported discussions, the scope of Goedhuis' space law recommendation was in the end expanded: the words *"and the legal nature of interplanetary space"* were added, thereby moving it away from the original air space and air law centric approach and creating the framework for discussions on many other aspects of the – future – use of space.

Though Goedhuis, at the 1958 New York Conference of the ILA, also played a role in the Air Law Committee as member of a Sub-Committee under Chauveau on the formation of an International Court of (Private) Air Law, as Rapporteur of his own Sub-Committee on "Air Sovereignty and the Legal Status of Outer Space" he concentrated on the preparation of a draft report, to be reviewed by his fellow-Sub-Committee members,[7] and to be discussed at the plenary meeting of the Air Law Committee.

6 The article that appeared on January 16, 2005 quoted him as follows: *"L'Organisation de l'aviation civile internationale (OACIOACI) estime que le temps est venu d'adopter des règlements pour assurer la protection des voyageurs et touristes spatiaux, une industrie qui pourrait littéralement prendre son essor d'ici cinq ans…Je ne vois rien d'autre que l'OACI pour mettre en place cette réglementation."* Both in 1956 and in 2005 the ICAO Secretariat produced papers on these matters but there was no further follow-up of substance.

7 Ambrosini, Garnault, Jennings, Lissitzyn, Meyer, and Pépin.

In the mean time, on 4 October 1957, Soviet Sputnik 1 had been launched, followed by the successful launch in February 1958 of the American Explorer 1 and other US satellites later in that year. It was only logical then that the debates in the Air Law Committee were lively and intense: the topicality of the issues and the importance of asking the right questions in order to find the right answers were beyond dispute.

Goedhuis took the approach which would become his preferred *modus operandi*: first describe the law as it exists, and then, if *lacunae* had been found as a result, formulate suggestions as to the legal regime that might be established, and, finally, submit draft resolutions to the Committee to focus the minds of the participants on reaching a common position. At all stages he would pay close attention to the views of other experts (whose ideas he always actively solicited) and he would not hesitate to make such amendments in the texts that he had originally proposed as were necessary to reach a consensus resolution.

The New York Conference apparently saw some participants doubting the need for ILA to occupy itself with the legal problems which might arise in connection with the use of outer space. The Report of the Conference shows a poetic side of Goedhuis when he makes the following remark:

> I have been informed that outer space is a place where during this Conference, some angels fear to tread – but if the wings of the angel of international cooperation through law – represented by our Association should be clipped and that angel would remain, therefore, earthbound, and not able to reach the higher regions of the atmosphere and beyond, a great opportunity would be lost.

In his "Recollections" he notes with gratitude about this episode that the great majority of the delegates were convinced of the highly important role the ILA would be able to play in the evolution of space law, and that a resolution was adopted which directed the Air Law Committee to continue its study of the legal problems relating to the status and use of space and which called upon the U.N. and other appropriate bodies to study the political, legal, economic, social and scientific problems involved in the utilization of outer space.

Those who participated in the debate, like Cooper, Bin Cheng, Myres McDougal, Alex Meyer, Lissitzyn, Lipson, Gorove and others did so with well-prepared solid presentations which showed their keen interest in the identification of existing rules and the creation of new principles guiding the use of outer space.

Bin Cheng may be singled out for two (arbitrary) reasons: he recalled with obvious delight that when appealing for a down-to-earth approach at another ILA session he was compared to the "Goofus bird" which always tried to fly backwards.[8] He did challenge with forceful arguments some of Goedhuis' *de lege lata* statements, but also approvingly repeated an earlier observation of Goedhuis in his Report: "[a]ll efforts to draw up a code of law before there is a clear realization of the national and international interests involved are bound to fail." One may conclude here that Goedhuis has learned from his many years as a diplomat and an aviation negotiator (confronted many times with the impact the concept of State sovereignty had on the dynamics of the airline industry) to be realistic when it comes to creating space law.
A good example is the question of the existence of (present) rules relating to the use of outer space. Goedhuis says the following in his Report:

> Can any conclusion be drawn from the attitude of States towards the placing in orbit of the Russian and American satellites? The U.S.S.R. and the U.S.A. have evidently acted on the premise that their rights to place their satellites in orbit for peaceful purposes is not dependent on the consent of any other State. The absence of protests against the satellites crossing the space above the territory of other States indicates a disinclination to claim sovereign rights.

And the "pioneer" resolution Goedhuis proposes at the end of his Report reads (in part):

> The International Law Association is of the opinion that outer space constitutes common property of mankind, open to use by all and not subject to appropriation by any one State, and calls upon the States to recognize this principle.

8 An – evidently more recent – Google search produces the following information about this mythical bird: "a bird distinctly low in intellectual curiosity, showing complete and consistent indifference as to where he is going. He prefers only to see where he has been, hence he always flies backwards."

Bin Cheng corrects him here: from that lack of protests can only be deduced "that States at present are content to acquiesce in such activities in their national air space. Moreover, States have generally given their blessings to the various research programmes of the International Geophysical Year of which the launching of satellites is merely one of the items." And when Goedhuis says that "insofar as freedom of passage is a necessary condition to the enjoyment of the benefits flowing from the use of outer space, such freedom should be recognized", Bin Cheng politely submits that perhaps the Rapporteur has merely intended to suggest the proposed freedoms as *lex ferenda*.

And Lissitzyn adds to that observation a statement made by the Legal Advisor of the Department of State in May 1958 before the Special Committee on Space and Astronautics of the U.S. Senate:

> (1) The [U.S.] has not recognized any upper limit to its sovereignty,
>
> (2) Failure to protest against the passage of satellites above the territory of the [U.S.] during the International Geophysical Year is based on an implied agreement, concluded only for the duration of that year, and does not constitute a precedent for the future.
>
> (3) The United States could rationally maintain that under the Chicago Convention the sovereignty of the United States extends 10,000 miles up, which may be the extent of the earth's atmosphere.
>
> (4) The United States has never conceded that it has no rights in the higher regions of space.
>
> (5) The United States does not concede that its activities in outer space do not entitle it to make a claim of sovereignty in outer space.

Lissitzyn concludes his quote of the official U.S. views with the observation that they indicate that there is considerable uncertainty as to the extent (read: delimitation) of air space for legal purposes and also that there is no agreement, as yet, on the principle that outer space is *res communis* or the common property of mankind.

It is clear from the above that Goedhuis' self-imposed task to report on the *lex lata* and make proposals *de lege ferenda* will force him to be realistic because of the national and international interests yet to be fully appreciated. He is aware of that and, through his *modus operandi* he invites, or rather forces, the participants to take a stand in the debate and try to come to a consensus on a (draft) ILA resolution and thus, cautiously, move forward. His above resolution proved a bridge too far and was amended to read – partly – as follows:

> Considering that the space lying beyond airspace should be utilised for peaceful purposes to the greatest common benefit of all mankind and that the recognition of this common interest should serve as the foundation of an international legal order for outer space.

At the Hamburg Conference in 1960, the topic on which Goedhuis reports is still called "Air sovereignty and the legal status of outer space", but the participants, influenced by the new (*Ad Hoc*) U.N. Committee on the Peaceful Uses of Outer Space and its Legal Committee in 1959, discuss many legal issues other than the already existing "Absence of agreement on the boundary between airspace and outer space" or the (non-)existence of a right of transit for space vehicles through air space.

In what is now called the Air and Space Law Committee, the tone of the Report and of the debate is different in another way: with the U.N. through the above Committees now fully involved in legal and *political* discussions on space law-to-be, the ILA participants note and comment on the work of those Committees and submit helpful ideas for consideration by those Committees: ILA does not (have to) create space law, the U.N. does.

When it comes to the dilemma of possible national claims vs. the free exploration and use of outer space and in particular of celestial bodies, Goedhuis proposes to use the Antarctic Treaty of December 1959 as a useful example of how to freeze the situation, thus creating time "for a gradual development of rules of law fitted to the needs and interest of the world community":

> No acts or activities taking place while the present Treaty is in force shall constitute a basis for asserting, supporting or denying a claim to territorial sovereignty in Antarctica or create any rights of sovereignty in Antarctica. No new claim, or enlargement of an existing claim [...] shall be asserted while the present Treaty is in force. (Art. 4 para. 2)

And he suggested to embrace another principle of the Antarctic Treaty, namely that "outer space shall be used for peaceful purposes only and that any measures of a military nature as well as the testing of any type of weapons shall be prohibited."

After the Hamburg Conference, Beaumont and Goedhuis, following the example of the IAF, agreed to divide the work of the Sub-Committee into four Working Groups, of which he would chair W.G. I: "General questions on the Legal Regime of Outer Space."[9] That topic enabled him to do what he felt most comfortable with: to report on and analyze trends in the political and legal thinking on the problems of outer space in the preceding years.

With the U.N. Outer Space Committee and its Legal Subcommittee increasingly active in this field, he could, at the August 1962 Conference in Brussels, report that the U.N. General Assembly had adopted its first resolution on international cooperation and the peaceful uses of outer space, Resolution 1721 A & B (XVI) of December 20, 1961. Observing that the U.N.G.A. Resolution confirmed two fundamental principles which had been the subject of the ILA Resolution as adopted at Hamburg (international law including the U.N. Charter applies to outer space, and outer space is free for exploration and use and not subject to national appropriation) he stated that: "the Association has every reason for satisfaction."

Noting the "sharp divergences of opinion" at the Legal Subcommittee in May/June 1962, he singled out three principles addressed in the U.N.G.A. Resolution on which the members could not find agreement, and discussed these at length in his Report to the Brussels Conference:

– Interpretation of the term "Outer Space"
– Interpretation of the term "Peaceful Uses"
– The applicability of International Law including the U.N. Charter

9 W.G. I: Chairman Goedhuis, members: Cheng, Cooper, Meyer, Zhukov; W.G. II (Space Technology and the Law of International Organization): Chairman Lipson, members: Ambrosini, Lissitzyn, Pépin; W.G. III (The Legal Status of Space Vehicles): Chairman Jennings, members: Chauveau, Huber, Nikolajevic; W.G. IV (Rules of Liability for Injury or Loss caused by the Operation of Space Vehicles): Chairman Berezowski, members: Garnault, Rinck, Roy.

The topics gave him the opportunity to once again argue in favor of a right, for space faring nations, of innocent transit for their satellites through foreign air space and to link this to the discussion on the interpretation of peaceful purposes (because, briefly, only "peaceful" satellites have a right of "innocent" passage). In the Legal Subcommittee, the U.S. and Soviet delegates discussed "peaceful uses" primarily in connection with the (il-)legality of operating spy satellites, with the U.S. and the U.K. taking the "peaceful means non aggressive" approach (and "espionage" is not a crime), and the Soviets and their colleagues speaking of "cosmic espionage" being criminal and inadmissible.

Here Goedhuis is hesitant to have ILA take a stand in this military-political debate, but, warning against ambiguous use of the term "peaceful" and quoting both the Antarctic Treaty and the Statute of the International Atomic Energy Agency concludes that "[b]oth agreements start from the correct premise that military purposes in general, defensive as well as offensive, are not "peaceful" purposes." Bin Cheng also warns that the U.S. interpretation "is likely to bring all rules and regulations based on the distinction between the peaceful and the military uses of outer space into disrepute."

Following a recommendation from the Air Law Committee at the Brussels Conference, a separate Space Law Committee was established with Goedhuis as chairman, to work in close cooperation with the Air Law Committee. The latter is understandable: with the rapid development of various space activities, more and more resulting legal issues have little to do with air space and air law; on the other hand, with *inter alia* the "definition and delimitation of outer space" question far from solved, sovereign air space and free outer space continued to meet both physically and legally.

The topics Goedhuis dealt with during his further years as chairman of the Space Law Committee reflect to a large extent the successive agendas of the annual sessions of the COPUOS Legal Subcommittee.[10] He paid particular

10 Satellite communications, direct broadcasting, remote sensing, liability, registration, military uses, definition/delimitation of outer space, rescue of astronauts & return of space objects, moon (resources), the legal status of U.N. resolutions/declarations on space, customary space law, etc. Prof. Maureen Williams, in a personal note, recalls: "The Committee for which he worked so much and in such style went through very important stages in the development of space law, particularly the issues of the Strategic Defense Initiative, the thorny confrontations with the

attention to the Equatorial States' challenge to the principle of freedom of use and non-appropriation of outer space in the form of the Bogotà Declaration and would again call for a definition/delimitation of outer space to put a definitive stop to this type of claims.

He would always see his ambitions as a lawyer aiming at regulating man's activities in space in perspective. As he said at the ILA Conference in 1962:

> The independence of us lawyers can never be more than relative. It is only a clear awareness of the political and social facts that enables us to play our role. The rules to be drafted regarding the legal regime of outer space must be based on a compromise between various requirements, among which the security requirements are certainly not the least important

In 1988, at the tender age of 83 – space law is a healthy pursuit, as other octogenarians and even older players in this branch of law may testify – he handed over his position of chairman to Prof. Dr. Karl-Heinz Böckstiegel of the Cologne Institute of Air and Space Law.

His colleagues paid tribute to him in a number of ways. Maureen Williams, reporting on the ILA Conference of the Space Law Committee in Queensland (1990):

> We have kept to the method and style chosen by our former Chairman, Professor Goedhuis, in his unforgettable task as such which extended over more than twenty years and indeed proved to be a major contribution to the development of the international law of outer space. (at p. 156)

And more recently, in an e-mail to one of the authors: "It was a real pleasure to work with Professor Goedhuis in this framework."

In 1996, at the Helsinki Conference, the Space Law Committee adopted the following tribute:

then U.S.S.R. on demilitarization, meetings between Gorbachov and Reagan, the 1976 Bogota Declaration where equatorial states demanded special rights over GEO, and the incipient commercial sides of space activities.

> The Space Law Committee hereby pays tribute to the memory of Professor Dr. Daniel Goedhuis (1905-1995) who chaired this Committee from its creation in 1960 until 1988 and indefatigably put his skill and efforts to the development of this new branch of International Law…

Bin Cheng, in his letter to one of the authors:

> The three resolutions which he proposed at the end of his report [for the 1958 New York Conference] were a clear indication of his clear and far-sighted vision of the state and development of space law, backed up by cogent arguments in his report.
>
> Through the turbulent debates on various aspects of space law, Daan produced reports after reports at successive ILA conferences analyzing in detail all the conflicting views both within his Sub-Committee and in the world at large, bearing in mind constantly all the latest technical developments, and always arriving at sound conclusions and making sensible proposals.
>
> Concurrent with the rapid and astonishing development of space activities, Daan's Committee under his leadership and drive also became a hive of activities in the study and advancement of the many aspects of space law, and it went from strength to strength.
>
> Daan's efforts were immense and his contribution to the subject highly enviable, and collaborating with him in the Space Law Committee and from the Air Law Committee was a pleasure and a privilege. He was a truly worthy pioneer in this field.

And Vladimir Kopal (in his letter to one of the authors of 8 August 2011), remembers meeting Goedhuis for the first time at the ILA Conference of 1956 in Dubrovnik; Kopal is then a young researcher. Contacts got closer in the 1980s. Goedhuis participated in a symposium organized by the U.N. University in The Hague in 1984 on "Maintaining outer space for peaceful purposes", to which he contributed a paper on "Legal implications of the present and projected military uses of outer space". After Kopal had become Chief of the U.N. Outer Space Affairs Division in 1985, Goedhuis invited him to join the Space Law Committee. Kopal participated in the work of that Committee ever since, inter alia by providing answers to the Questionnaires that Goedhuis regularly sent out. On Goedhuis he remarks:

> Professor Daniel Goedhuis was a nice man, both physically and spiritually. Always elegant – he liked a dark blue colour for his suits-, he was very polite, tolerant and friendly in his contacts with other people. His scholarly views always deserved to be carefully studied. In many space law issues, I found similarities with my own approach. By his constructive views and organizational efforts, Professor Goedhuis essentially contributed to the developing and strengthening of the rule of law in space.

Prof. Maarten Bos, in his *in memoriam* in the Netherlands International Law Review:

> In him, one of the world's first and finest experts in air and space law passed away, a man to whom the epithet of inspirator and originator fully seems to apply and who, in time, will be recognized as part of legal history – a rare and enviable title few others can claim.[...] Goedhuis had an open eye for the unprecedented ways of law-creation as practiced under the pressure of a fast-growing space technology. [...] With regard to the technological aspects involved, he always provided proof of astonishing insight.[...] we may be sure that his role was a pioneering one, and that for all time to come he will have his place in the long line of eminent international lawyers to which his home country gave birth.

Goedhuis' 1989 article in the Netherlands International Law Review, titled "Reflections on some of the main problems arising in the future development of space law" may be regarded as his "swan song". In that article, Goedhuis reviews the "present ambiguous and most significant legal rules", on the meaning and content of which no consensus has been reached so far: rules related to the definition of outer space, including the right of innocent passage for space craft through foreign air space, the application of the non-appropriation provision to natural resources, direct broadcasting, remote sensing and "the crucial issue of military space applications which overshadows all others in the space environment." He lists two factors which prevented the reaching of a consensus:

> First, at the present stage of space development, States are still to a considerable extent uncertain of how these developments will affect their political, economic and military national interests, and second, a great unawareness still exists

> among States of how the unique characteristics of the conquest of space … have changed their national interests (at 252).

This quote reflects Goedhuis' realistic approach to the development of space law: without awareness of technological and political developments and their – possible – effect on national interest, and vice versa, it is impossible to develop law. In that sense he would have been highly interested in analyzing and discussing the prospects for an international regulation of space debris mitigation because of the shared interest of all space faring nations, and their satellite users, in orbits free of satellite threatening space junk.

Finally, mention should be made of two organizations that benefitted from his dedication to space law *in statu nascendi*. In 1970, at the invitation of Charles S. Ryne, American President of the World Peace Through Law Centre, he became chairman of the Centre's Sub-committee on the peaceful uses of outer space. In that position he presented papers at two conferences, the last one in Manila in 1977, where a resolution was adopted that the principles of freedom and non-appropriation of outer space were rules of positive international law independent of any treaty; the Bogotà Declaration was a hotly debated issue in those days! He resigned from his position in the mid-1980s because, as he said in his "Recollections", he perceived the organization's approach as too American-centered "without considering how the rules of space might be developed to the benefit of the world community in general.

The *Académie de Droit International de la Haye* (Hague Academy of International law) asked him three times, to lecture for its international student audience at the Peace Palace in the Hague. The texts of his air and space law courses, which were popular and well-attended, have been published in the Academy's *Receuil des Cours* under the following headings:

- "Questions of Public International Air Law"
- "Conflicts of law and divergencies in the legal regimes of air space and outer space" and
- "The problems of the frontiers of outer space and air space."[11]

11 *Questions of public international air law*, 81 Recueil des Cours 201-307 (1952); *Conflicts of law and divergencies in the legal regimes of air space and outer space*, 109 Recueil des Cours 257-346 (1963); *The problems of the frontiers of outer space and air space*, 174 Recueil des Cours 367-407 (1982).

F. Goedhuis as Teacher

Goedhuis enjoyed his two-weekly trips from London to Leiden to teach. It goes without saying that, as from the late 1950s, he added space law to his existing air law curriculum. In 1961, the year that his aviation (negotiating) work for the Dutch government officially stopped, Leiden University became the first such institution in the world to create a Chair of Air and Space Law. The contents of his lectures and his publications reflected this shift in teaching tasks.

Since he was appointed Professor of Air Law in 1947, a limited number of *promovendi* defended doctoral dissertations on air law, the last one, in 1957, being his successor as an aviation negotiator and in 1977 as Professor at Leiden University, Henri Wassenbergh, with a topic with which Goedhuis was no doubt familiar: "Post-War International Civil Aviation Policy and the Law of the Air." And in 1975, Mr. Ogunsola O. Ogunbanwo of Nigeria got his doctorate of law with a thesis entitled "International Law and Outer Space Activities".

The course he offered at Leiden was an optional one, selected by students in the last phase/year of their law studies. Most would opt for a more down-to-earth course, offering better job opportunities than the rather exotic subject of air and/or space law seemed to promise at the time. Some were fascinated by this relatively new field of law and benefitted from his knowledge and experience. Toshio Kosuge and Peter van Fenema were his only students in the academic year 1968/1969 (at the end of which Neil Armstrong set foot on the moon!), and would, every fortnight, eagerly await his arrival by taxi from the airport to listen to his always well-prepared lecture, alternate in Dutch and English. Immaculately dressed in a Savile Row suit – an unusual outfit for professors in the late 1960s even in rather formal Leiden – and with an elegant hairstyle, he would graciously offer his two students tea and cake during the break and converse on space law with those present: the small group did stick out in the crowd!

Prof. Kosuge, who stayed more years in the Netherlands and got married in that country, fondly recalls the highly topical lectures and the pleasant teaching and personal style of his professor at the time, including the trips he made to London to get his advice on the space law research he performed. They kept in touch long after Kosuge's return to Japan.

Other students recall praying to be invited to London for their oral examination: in that case Goedhuis would pay for the ticket, the exam would take place in the Netherlands Embassy, and the successful candidate would be able to immerse in London's nightlife to celebrate the end of his or her student years in style.

In 1975 Goedhuis retired as professor; in his March 1977 farewell lecture "The legal regime of outer space: between yesterday and tomorrow" he paid particular attention to the need for international cooperation and the role of public opinion when it comes to mitigating the negative influences on the development of space law caused by the exercise of national power, by the conflicts between "haves" and "have-nots" and by possible military escalation. When referring to the U.N. space law-making activities he quoted Grotius, who in a 1614 letter to a friend wrote: "Let us plant trees for the benefit of those who come after us."

When he died twenty years later, he had certainly done his fair share of contributing to that effort.

Chapter VIII **Eilene M. Galloway** (4.5.1906 – 2.5.2009)

Marcia S. Smith* and Jonathan F. Galloway**

A. Introduction

On October 4, 1957, the day that the launch of Sputnik by the Soviet Union opened the Space Age, Eilene Marie Galloway was a national defense expert

* Marcia S. Smith is President of Space and Technology Policy Group, LLC, and founder and editor of SpacePolicyOnline.com. Eilene Galloway was her mentor and dear friend for more than 30 years. She also spent a large portion of her career (1975-2006) as a space policy specialist at the Congressional Research Service (CRS), arriving at CRS the same year that Dr. Galloway retired. Ms. Smith retired from CRS in 2006 and became Director of the Space Studies Board and the Aeronautics and Space Engineering Board at the U.S. National Academy of Sciences, leaving in 2009 to start her own consulting firm and website. She was Vice President of the International Institute of Space Law (IISL) from 2003-2006 and is a Fellow of the American Institute of Aeronautics and Astronautics and of the American Astronautical Society, and a member and former Trustee of the International Academy of Astronautics.

** Jonathan F. Galloway is Eilene's son. She gave him the idea for his Ph.D. dissertation at Columbia University (1967) which was published as *The Politics and Technology of Satellite Communications* (Heath Lexington Books, 1972). He taught International Relations at Lake Forest College in Illinois from 1966 to 2002. He retired as Professor Emeritus on the Irwin L. & Fern D. Young Presidential Chair. He has served as Vice President of the International Institute of Space Law since 2006. He is Co-chair of the Space Law Committee of the American Branch of the International Law As-

Stephan Hobe (ed.), Pioneers of Space Law
© 2013 International Institute of Space Law. ISBN *978-90-04-24027-8. pp. 127-149*

for the United States Congress. Working for the Legislative Reference Service (LRS, later renamed the Congressional Research Service), a department of the Library of Congress, her responsibility was providing objective, non-partisan research and analysis exclusively for the Members and committees of Congress.

After joining LRS in 1941, she had risen through the ranks developing expertise on national security issues including the emerging field of ballistic missiles and their implications for U.S. security. She worked particularly closely with the chairman of the Senate Armed Services Committee, Senator Richard Russell, so it was natural that after Sputnik was launched Russell and Senate Majority Leader Senator Lyndon B. Johnson (LBJ) turned to Eilene for assistance in deciding how the United States should respond.

As she would remark for the rest of her career, the launch of Sputnik initially incited fear and alarm in the United States. LBJ (later Vice President and then President of the United States), established a special Senate Subcommittee on Preparedness to investigate and study the implications.

A political scientist, Eilene assisted in preparing hearings held by the subcommittee and drafting legislation that ultimately became the National Aeronautics and Space Act of 1958 (NASA Act). It created the National Aeronautics and Space Administration (NASA) to conduct U.S. civil space activities while assigning the conduct of military space activities to the Department of Defense (DOD).

She was also closely involved in the U.S. role in formation of the U.N. Committee on Peaceful Uses of Outer Space (COPUOS) and the formation and evolution of the International Institute of Space Law (IISL) and International Academy of Astronautics (IAA). Those were important neutral venues for discussions about space activities at the height of the Cold War.

A central tenet of Eilene's efforts was ensuring that international cooperation in space was an integral part of the U.S. civil space program. She also fought to ensure that discussions about the future of space activities involved not only science and engineering, but legal and policy experts. Eilene was

sociation and is also a member of the International Academy of Astronautics, the American Society of International Law and the American Institute of Aeronautics and Astronautics.

adamant that inclusive debate and consensus building would lead to outer space being used for peaceful purposes and for the benefit of all humankind.

Eilene died on May 2, 2009, two days shy of her 103rd birthday. For the 52 years between the launch of Sputnik and her passing, Eilene maintained her steadfast belief that space activities unify the countries of the world. Her passions were avoiding the placement of weapons in outer space, supporting human exploration of the solar system, and ensuring international cooperation.

She is a pioneer in the creation of the field of space law through her work with the U.S. Congress in drafting laws and her involvement in the international institutions where the international law of outer space has been formed. Examples of her influence can be found in three aspects of the NASA Act that created NASA and assigned military space activities to the Department of Defense – the decision to organize NASA as an Administration instead of an Agency, section 201 that created a National Aeronautics and Space Council in the White House to coordinate space activities across the U.S. government, and inclusion of section 205 that encouraged NASA to engage in international cooperation – as well as in the U.S. role in creating COPUOS.

B. Early Life and Career

Born Eilene Marie Slack on May 4, 1906 in Kansas City, Missouri, Eilene was a top student and avid member of her high school's debate team.

She won a full scholarship to Washington University in St. Louis, Missouri at the age of 17. The scholarship covered only tuition, however, and Eilene needed to work to earn living expenses. Very soon after arriving at college in 1923, she accepted a secretarial position that included typing the dissertation of a student named George Barnes Galloway. It was love at first sight, and the two married in 1924.

George Galloway entered the Ph.D. program in Political Science at the Brookings Institution, which was then located at Washington University. Brookings decided to relocate to Washington, D.C. In 1924, George moved to Washington while Eilene remained in St. Louis for her sophomore year. She then joined George and they moved to Philadelphia, Pennsylvania where George took a job with the Philadelphia Bureau of Municipal Research. Eilene continued her studies at Swarthmore College where they welcomed their first son, David, in 1927.

In 1928, Eilene received a bachelor's degree Phi Beta Kappa in Political Science from Swarthmore and became an instructor at the college while George continued to work in Philadelphia. Their lives changed dramatically on October 29, 1929, however, with the stock market crash and the ensuing Great Depression. Both lost their jobs and all their savings, forcing them to move in with George's parents in Passaic, New Jersey. Eilene was able to find work as a secretary in the brand new Empire State Building in nearby New York City, but it was more difficult for George.

After a brief stint working for Governor Pinchot in Harrisburg, Pennsylvania, Eilene and George moved back to Washington, D.C. At the beginning of the Franklin Delano Roosevelt administration, George obtained a position at the National Recovery Administration while Eilene landed a job at the Federal Emergency Relief Administration. When these positions ended in two years, George received a grant from a wealthy philanthropist. The task was to travel to every state and the border regions of Mexico and Canada and write a report on how the Great Depression affected people from all walks of life.

After placing eight-year-old David with close family friends, Eilene and George set out on a one-year trek, visiting every state except Nevada, as well as portions of Mexico and the Canadian province of British Columbia. George wrote his notes and Eilene typed them every day, as well as typing her own reflections on what they observed.

Upon returning to the nation's capital, George held a series of research positions with the National Planning Association and the American Political Science Association. And, in 1939, the family grew as a second son, Jonathan, was born. Later, George became staff director of the LaFollette-Monroney Committee which produced the Legislative Reorganization Act which President Harry S. Truman signed in 1946. Also, during this period, the family bought what would be Eilene's home in the upper northwest portion of the city for the rest of her life. And, in 1946, George became a Senior Specialist in American National Government at the Legislative Reference Service (LRS) with a specialty in how Congress operates.

Eilene worked in several positions in Washington, D.C. during that time, and in 1941 became an LRS researcher herself. One of her reports, "Atomic Power: the Issues Before Congress," was written for Senator Brian McMahon, Chairman of the Joint Committee on Atomic Energy, and helped establish her as an authority on national security issues. She steadily climbed the ranks of the LRS and by 1957 was a specialist in national defense working with the highest ranking members of the House of Representatives and the Senate on national security issues.

C. Career in Space Law and Policy

1. *Drafting the 1958 National Aeronautics and Space Act*

In mid-1957, Eilene was working for LRS providing policy analysis to Senators and Representatives on a variety of military issues. A particularly notable report she wrote at the time was entitled "Guided Missiles in Foreign Countries," which was published jointly by the Armed Services Committees in the House and Senate.

October 4, 1957, the day Sputnik launched the Space Age, was a Friday. As Eilene told the story, the next Monday she received a call from Senate Majority Leader Lyndon B. Johnson (LBJ) asking for her assistance in determining how the United States should react to this development. In 1992, she recounted:

> Sputnik exploded on Capital [sic] Hill like a psychological bomb, arousing fears of orbiting weapons and consternation that the Soviet Union had taken the lead in rocketry. The general public reacted with alarm.[1]

1 NASA. Legislative Origins of the National Aeronautics and Space Act of 1958: Proceedings of an Oral History Workshop Conducted Apr. 3, 1992. Monographs *in* Aerospace History Number 8. NASA, Washington, D.C., 1998 (hereinafter Legislative Origins). The law is officially called National Aeronautics and Space Act of 1958. Public Law 85-568. 72 Stat. 426. Now it is in Title 51 of the United States Code. During the workshop, which was moderated by Dr. John Logsdon of George Washington University, Galloway recounted her involvement with the drafting of the NASA Act. She also wrote an appendix to the report providing further details of Senator Johnson's reaction to Sputnik's launch.

a. Senate Hearings on Preparedness: Turning Fear of War Into Hope for Peace

As she helped LBJ organize and conduct hearings for the Senate Preparedness Investigating Subcommittee of the Senate Armed Services Committee in response to Sputnik's launch, Eilene herself was learning about the space program and its implications in both the scientific and military spheres. She often joked that on the day LBJ called her "the only thing I knew about space was that the cow jumped over the Moon."[2]

The Senate Preparedness Subcommittee began hearings on November 25, 1957. Eilene would recall in later years that during the hearings "[f]ear of war changed to hope for peace"[3] as Senators heard from scientists engaged in the International Geophysical Year (IGY) about the scientific benefits of space exploration. Although Sputnik certainly took place in the context of the superpower rivalry between the Soviet Union and the United States, both countries had committed to launching satellites to support the IGY and both did.[4] The IGY was organized by scientists from 60 countries to conduct coordinated studies of geophysical phenomena between July 1, 1957 and December 31, 1958.

It was during these hearings that Eilene began her contacts and friendships in what became known as the space law community. On December 31, 1958, at LBJ's request, she joined together in one Senate volume the early writings of Andrew Haley, John Cobb Cooper, C. Wilfred Jenks, Eugene Pepin, Isabella Diederiks-Verschoor (then de Rode-Verschoor), and Bin Cheng

2 Eilene Galloway, the Woman who Helped Create NASA, Dies at Age 102. NASA website. Available at http://www.nasa.gov/topics/history/features/galloway_obit.html, visited Mar. 26, 2012. The reference is to a nursery rhyme: "Hew diddle diddle, the cat and the fiddle, the cow jumped over the Moon. The little dog laughed to see such sport and the dish ran away with the spoon."

3 Eilene Galloway. Sputnik and the Creation of NASA: A Personal Perspective. In: NASA: 50 Years of Exploration and Discovery. NASA, 2007. Available at http://www.nasa.gov/50th/50th_magazine/50years.html

4 The United States launched its first orbiting satellite, Explorer I, on Jan. 31, 1958 GMT.

among many other early pioneers in the field of space law.[5] A second volume came out in 1961 including other space pioneers such as Alex Meyer, Vladimir Kopal, Gyula Gal, Yevgeny Korovin and Martin Menter.[6] When these and like documents were published over the ensuing years, she sent copies to her colleagues all around the world.

b. International Cooperation in Space: Section 205 of the National Aeronautics and Space Act

Eilene's enthusiasm for and dedication to international cooperation in the new arena of space activities emerged from these hearings. As she helped the Senate and House draft their versions of legislation about how the government should organize for space activities,[7] she argued convincingly for including what became section 205 of the 1958 National Aeronautics and Space Act.[8] In recounting her role in writing that law, she revealed that at the final meeting of Senators where agreement was made to include Section 205,

5 U.S. Congress. Senate. Special Committee on Space and Astronautics. Space Law: A Symposium. 85th Congress, Second Session. Washington. D.C., U.S. Government Printing Office. Dec. 31, 1958.

6 U.S. Congress. Senate. Committee on Aeronautical and Space Sciences. Legal Problems of Space Exploration: A Symposium. 87th Congress, First Session. Doc. 26. Washington, D.C., U.S. Government Printing Office, Mar. 22, 1961.

7 Formulation of legislation in the United States involves a plethora of actors. Often, the President will draft a law he hopes Congress will pass. The U.S. House of Representatives and the U.S. Senate each develop their own drafts (using the President's draft as input), pass them, and then work together to reach agreement on a final version that is then returned to the President for signature (or veto). This is the path that the National Aeronautics and Space Act took, and Eilene worked with the leadership of both the House and the Senate as they developed their drafts and reached agreement on the final law.

8 Section 205 (1) (now 51 U.S.C. 20115) reads "The Administration, under the foreign policy guidance of the President, may engage in a program of international cooperation in work done pursuant to this chapter, and in the peaceful application of the results thereof, pursuant to agreements made by the President with the advice and consent of the Senate."

a Senator who apparently had fallen asleep suddenly awakened and said that the law should include a requirement that NASA's international agreements obtain the advice and consent of the Senate. That would make international agreements akin to treaties. Eilene reacted with alarm and determination to find a way to ameliorate the situation.

> Well, I was absolutely stunned and very, very upset, because I knew that NASA could not have a program of international cooperation if everyone had to come to the Senate. So I spoke to Senator Johnson about this, and he said it was all right for me to tell Herbert Reis, was who in the Office of Legal Affairs of the State Department, of my concern. I think it must have been Herbert Reis who wrote the [signing] statement by President Eisenhower, who said that this section does not preclude less formal arrangements.[9]

A few years later, when some Senators expressed concern about NASA's co-operative activities, Eilene wrote a document[10] for the Senate laying out all the types of international cooperation in which NASA was engaged showing that "there are a lot of things that you can do internationally that do not require an Executive agreement or a treaty." [11] She was always emphasizing the peaceful uses and benefits of space endeavors; she carried around a little booklet of NASA's international programs with over a hundred countries in such fields as communication satellites, meteorological satellites and earth resource programs.

9 Legislative Origins, *supra* note 1 at 34.

10 U.S. Congress. Senate. Committee on Aeronautical and Space Sciences. United States International Space Programs: Texts of Executive Agreements, Memoranda of Understanding and Other International Arrangements 1959-1965. 89th Congress, 1st Session. U.S. Government Printing Office, Washington, D.C., July, 1965. 575 pages.

11 Legislative Origins, *supra* note 1 at 34.

c Interagency Coordination: Section 201 of the National Aeronautics and Space Act

As a national defense analyst at LRS, Eilene was extremely familiar with the problems of coordination between government agencies, especially civilian agencies and the Department of Defense, as well as rivalries within and between them. In this connection, she pushed for the establishment of a National Aeronautics and Space Council (NASC) within the White House, chaired by the President himself. The members of the council were the Secretary of State, the Secretary of Defense, the Administrator of NASA, the Chairman of the Atomic Energy Commission and four other members to be appointed by the President. Congress included the NASC as section 201 of the NASA Act.[12] Strong interagency relationships would be necessary, Eilene knew, before the United States could cooperate with foreign countries.

d. NASA as an Administration Instead of an Agency

When President Eisenhower sent his draft of the bill to Congress, NASA was called the National Aeronautics and Space Agency. At that time, Representative John McCormack was Speaker of the House of Representatives (the top position in the House, and third in line of presidential succession) and asked Eilene for her advice as he reviewed the draft legislation. One point that particularly concerned Eilene was that within the U.S. Government structure, agencies had less stature than administrations, especially when dealing with other parts of the government. She knew that NASA would have to work closely with the Department of Defense and Department of State and

12 *Id.* at 32-33. President John F. Kennedy designated LBJ, by then his Vice President, to chair the Council and it remained a part of the White House, chaired by the Vice President, until it was abolished by President Nixon in 1973. Congress recreated the Council, without the aeronautics component, in the 1989 NASA Authorization Act. The White House National Space Council was chaired by Vice President Daniel Quayle during the George H.W. Bush presidency. Subsequent presidents have chosen not to fund or staff the space council, so although it still exists in law, from a practical standpoint it does not exist. The interagency coordination problems still do.

convinced McCormack that it should be an administration. The Speaker immediately had his clerk cross out "agency" and insert "administration" in each case throughout the draft bill. That is the version that passed the House and was included in the bill as enacted. Thus we have the National Aeronautics and Space Administration, which interacts with other government entities on a more equal footing.[13]

2. *U.N. Committee on Peaceful Uses of Outer Space*

LBJ, at President Dwight D. Eisenhower's request, represented the United States at the United Nations in discussions to create the ad hoc (now permanent) Committee on Peaceful Uses of Outer Space (COPUOS). Eilene often remarked at how the fact that a Republican President asked a Democratic Senator to lead the U.S. delegation demonstrated from the very beginning that the space program transcended partisan politics and unified the country.

Working from LBJ's ranch in Texas, Eilene and a small group of other congressional staff worked with LBJ to draft the speech. President Eisenhower sent a plane to take them all to New York and LBJ delivered the speech on November 17, 1958.

Speaking for the Senate and referencing the agreement of the House of Representatives, LBJ said, in language clearly reflecting Eilene's input, "... we of the United States see one course – and only one – which the nations of earth may intelligently pursue. That is the course of full and complete and immediate cooperation to make the exploration of outer space a joint adventure."[14] In 1992, Eilene reflected on this optimistic occasion:

> We had nineteen other countries lined up. Johnson made this speech in which he said outer space is unscarred by conflict, it must remain peaceful. It must be an arena for peace. This was really an exciting moment because this led the United

13 *Id.* at 33.

14 Statement by Senator Lyndon B. Johnson, in Committee One, on Outer Space. United States Mission to the United Nations. Press Release #3081. Nov. 17, 1958. From these pioneering beginnings came forth the work of COPUOS including the five outer space treaties!

> Nations to adopt the ad hoc Committee on the Peaceful Uses of Outer Space. Within a year the Soviet Union, Czechoslovakia and Poland had decided to go in with us. We had decided by that time to make all the decisions by consensus instead of voting.[15]

3. *International Institute of Space Law and International Academy of Astronautics*

Meanwhile, also in 1958 on the international stage, the first colloquium on space law was being organized at The Hague. LBJ decided at the last minute that Eilene should participate in the colloquium and arranged for Eilene to be accommodated on a military aircraft to get her to Europe in time. She gaily would tell the story later of how the airplane landed to refuel in the Azores and everyone was invited to disembark and enjoy a small repast. She was weary and declined, but was then told that she had been given the temporary rank of a four-star general and no one could leave the plane until she did.

She immediately reconsidered and joined everyone, of course, but it was just the beginning of an amazing journey that led to a lifelong association with IISL and close friendships with IISL leaders including Isabella Diederiks-Verschoor of the Netherlands, Eugene Pepin of France, Manfred Lachs of Poland, Nandasiri Jasentuliyana of Sri Lanka, Tanja Masson-Zwaan of the Netherlands and Gennady P. Zhukov and Vladlen S. Vereshchetin of the Soviet Union/Russia. At that colloquium, Eilene presented a paper entitled "The Community of Law and Science,"[16] the first of dozens of IISL papers she wrote over the decades.

One of her strongest convictions was that issues in space law and policy required an interdisciplinary approach that brought together not only science and engineering, but social science fields, including law. She became

15 Legislative Origins, *supra* note 1 at 35. On her views on consensus voting, *see* Eilene Galloway. *Consensus as a Basis for International Space Cooperation.* 20TH COLLOQUIUM ON THE LAW OF OUTER SPACE. Prague, Czechoslovakia, 1977, 105-111.

16 Eilene Galloway. *The Community of Law and Science. in*: FIRST COLLOQUIUM ON THE LAW OF OUTER SPACE. THE HAGUE. 1958. PROCEEDINGS. Edited by Andrew G. Haley and Dr. Welf Heinrich, Prince of Hanover. Paris, International Institute of Space Law (Original Printing – Wien – Springer -Verlag – 1959). 59-62.

very closely involved with the International Academy of Astronautics (IAA), building a consensus to create a new "Section 4"[17] specifically for social science and a standing committee on Space Activities and Society, which she chaired for many years.

4. *The 1960's and Early 1970's*

Eilene continued working for LRS through the 1960s and the first half of the 1970s. LRS became the Congressional Research Service (CRS) in 1970, by which time Eilene had been promoted to its highest level, a Senior Specialist.

She assisted, in particular, the Senate committee with oversight over civilian space activities (originally the Senate Aeronautical and Space Science Committee, which was abolished and its jurisdiction absorbed into the new Commerce, Science, and Transportation Committee) as it promulgated the Communications Satellite Act of 1962 and oversaw the development of the first four U.N. space treaties, all of which required the Senate's advice and consent to ratification.

Her husband, George, passed away in 1967, just one year after retiring from CRS. Eilene focused on her work and the growing number of Galloway grandchildren.[18] Her list of congressional and non-congressional publications grew, expanding her influence in the debates over space law and policy. She was an official observer at many meetings of COPUOUS, reporting back to the Senate on what transpired there.

D. Post-Congressional Career

Eilene retired from CRS in 1975, but remained vigorously involved in space law and policy for the next 34 years. In addition to serving on many advisory committees and in official positions for the IISL and IAA, she also continued to consult for Congress. In particular, she wrote an analysis of the Moon Treaty in May 1980 for the Senate Commerce, Science, and Transportation

17 The other three sections are for space science, space engineering and space life sciences.

18 At the time of her death, she had six grandchildren and five great-grandchildren.

Committee,[19] and the introduction to a compendium of space law documents published by the same committee in 1990.[20]

1. *Analysis of the Moon Agreement for the Senate*

Under the U.S. Constitution, the Senate must provide advice and consent on the ratification of treaties. In 1980, she was asked by the Senate Commerce, Science and Transportation Committee to provide an analysis of the U.N. Agreement Governing the Activities of States on the Moon and Other Celestial Bodies (the Moon Agreement).

In her analysis, in addition to outlining its negotiating history, she raised a number of issues that still contribute to the understanding and development of space law and are witness to Eilene's foresight. For instance, she writes "What are the provisions of the Moon Agreement which go beyond the space treaties already in force? Do they appreciably offer positive guidelines for the future development of space industrialization? What does this term (the "Common Heritage of Mankind") add to the 'province of all mankind' provided in Article 4 of the Agreement?" And "What can be done about the uneven membership of States in the total body of space law that has been developed?"[21]

2. *Arms Control in Outer Space and the Hague Symposium*

Given Eilene Galloway's history as a student of military affairs and national defense at the LRS, it was natural for her to continue her analyses of arms

19 U.S. Senate. Committee on Commerce, Science and Transportation. Agreement Governing the Activities of States on the Moon and Other Celestial Bodies, Parts 1 and 2. Committee Print. 96th Congress, 2nd Session. Washington, D.C., U.S. Government Printing Office, May, 1980. (hereinafter Moon Agreement Committee Print).

20 U.S. Senate. Committee on Commerce, Science and Transportation. Space Law and Related Documents. 101st Congress, 2nd Session. S. Print. 101-98. Washington, D.C., U.S. Government Printing Office, June 1990.

21 U.S. Senate. Agreement Governing the Activities of States on the Moon and Other Celestial Objects, *supra* note 20 at 78-80.

control in outer space, which had been started by the Partial Test Ban Treaty of 1963[22] which bans atomic testing in outer space and by Article IV of the Outer Space Treaty[23] which bans the orbiting of weapons of mass destruction. In 1982, she gave a paper at the 25th Colloquium on the Law of Outer Space in Paris, France in which she argued for expanding Article IV of the 1967 Outer Space Treaty.[24] She feared a space arms race. Military projects of reconnaissance and communications and other defensive applications should be continued, she agreed, but there should be a ban on weapons in outer space.

One activity of which she was especially proud was organizing a symposium at The Hague on Conditions Essential for Maintaining Outer Space for Peaceful Purposes. The March 12-13, 1984 symposium was sponsored by the International Institute of Space Law and the United Nations University in Cooperation with the Peace Palace and the Hague Carnegie Foundation. She would often say that she had been contemplating complete retirement and moving to Florida, but reconsidered when asked to organize this symposium, for which she was very grateful since it led to so many more years of activity in the field she loved.

3. *Other Activities As She Reached Her Centenary*

She remained very active with IISL and IAA, attending most of the IISL colloquia and IAA meetings held as part of the annual International Astronautical Congresses through 2002, almost always presenting papers on topical issues. She was a long-term member of the IISL Board and she was elected an Honorary Director when she stepped down from her Board position. She chaired the IAA Space Activities and Society Committee and was an IAA Trustee for many years. In 1995, IAA adopted a new membership category

22 Treaty Banning Nuclear Weapons Tests in the Atmosphere, in Outer Space and Under Water. (1963) 14 UST 1313; TIAS 5433: 480 UNTS 43.

23 Treaty on the Principles Governing the Activities of States in the Exploration and Use of Outer Space, including the Moon and Other Celestial Bodies. (1967) 18 UST 2410; TIAS 6347; 610 UNTS 205.

24 Eilene M. Galloway. Expanding Article IV of the 1967 Space Treaty: A Proposal. Proceedings of the 25th Colloquium on the Law of Outer Space. Reston, Virginia. AIAA. 1983. 89-92.

of Trustee Emeritus to which Eilene was elected. She also served on NASA advisory committees, including NASA's Space Station Advisory Committee.

In 2001, at the age of 95, Dr. Galloway was invited by Prof. Dr. Karl-Heinz Böckstiegel to attend a colloquium on space law at the Institute of Air and Space Law at the University of Cologne. There, her knowledge of history and her insights into the future were apparent in her analyses of these aspects of international space law: the contributions of the IGY to space science and the development of international cooperation; whether there should be a fixed boundary between air space and outer space; what developments in space law are customary international law; the geostationary orbit as a limited natural resource; the relationship between equality and equity vis-à-vis the sharing of the peaceful benefits of space exploration; the ICAO (International Civil Aviation Organization) as a model for managing space air traffic control; controlling space debris; the development of global navigation satellite systems; and the role of arms control and the military in outer space. [25]

On the occasion of her 100th birthday in 2006, Representative Bart Gordon, chair of the Science Committee of the U.S. House of Representatives, paid tribute to Eilene for her "life of distinguished service to this Nation and her profession.... Throughout her professional career, Dr. Galloway has been an influential force in the development and analysis of domestic and international space policy and law."[26]

E. Final Publications and Enduring Influence

Eilene published her last op-ed piece, "Space Law for the Moon and Mars," in the trade publication Space News five weeks before her death on May 2, 2009.[27]

25 *Law for Space Activities in the 21st Century in*: Air and Space Law in the 21st Century, eds. Marietta Benkö and Walter Kröll. Institute of Air and Space Law of the University of Cologne, Germany, 2001, 326-338.

26 Representative Bart Gordon. In Honor of Dr. Eilene Galloway's 100th Birthday. Congressional Record, May 16, 2006, E838. Washington, U.S. Government Printing Office, 2006.

27 Eilene Galloway. Space Law for the Moon/Mars Mission, Space News, March 2009, 33.

Her final writing, the preface to volume 1 of the Commentary on Space Law (CoCoSL), was published posthumously.[28]

Ambassador Peter Jankowitsch, who chaired COPUOS for more than a decade, was among the many leaders in space policy and law who paid tribute to Eilene after her death. He said:

> During my whole tenure of the UN Committee on the Peaceful Uses of Outer Space (and of course thereafter) Eilene Galloway was a constant source of inspiration and motivation and was certainly always first amongst those who guided and helped our work. ... Her devotion to the idea of the rule of law in Outer Space is at the root of many of the advances that space law has seen over the years and she will be an important and helpful point of reference for future space legislators.[29]

Andrei Terekhov, Executive Director, Office of Administration of Justice at the United Nations, commented that "Her contribution to the establishment and development of the law of outer space cannot be overstated."[30]

Judge Vladen Vereshchetin, a pioneer in space law himself and a Member of the International Court of Justice from 1995-2006, said that "Eilene Galloway's lasting and passionate devotion to the cause of international space cooperation and to the development of legal regulation of space activity has forever gained her respect and affection of the world space community."[31]

Former IISL President Nandasiri Jasentuliyana dedicated his seminal book *Space Law: Development and Scope* to Eilene – "For her lifelong contribution to space law."[32]

28 Eilene Galloway. Preface to Volume 1. Cologne Commentary on Space Law (CoCoSL). Vol. 1: Outer Space Treaty. Edited by Stephan Hobe, Bernhard Schmidt-Tedd and Kai-Uwe Schrogl. Assistant editor Gerardine Meishan Goh. Cologne, Carl Heymanns Verlag, 2009, p. xix.

29 Peter Jankowitsch. Tribute to Eilene M. Galloway. Published on the website of the International Institute of Space Law (IISL), visited April 21, 2012.

30 IISL website, *Id.*

31 IISL website, *Id.*

32 Nandasiri, Jasentuliyana, ed. Space Law: Development and Scope. Westport CT and London, Praeger, 1992.

Perhaps most importantly, she was a mentor to many young women and men all around the world who have a deep and abiding interest in space law and space policy. There are so many of these students of outer space and the cosmos that we cannot name them all, but we can say that Eilene was in contact with scholars, lawyers and policy makers from all over the globe who are aged from their 30s to their 90s. She loved to tell stories. Talking with her in her living room was the same as attending an advanced seminar in the history of the personalities, policies and laws of the space age. She radiated warmth, optimism and a great joie de vivre.

She is indeed a pioneer of space law.

F. Honors and Awards

Eilene was awarded an Honorary Doctor of Laws degree from Lake Forest College in 1990 and another Honorary Doctor of Laws degree from Swarthmore College, her alma mater, in 1992.

A small sampling of her many other honors and awards includes the following:

- Honored by the annual Eilene M. Galloway Symposium on Critical Issues in Space Law in Washington, D.C. established in 2006 by the IISL and The National Center for Remote Sensing, Air and Space Law at the University of Mississippi School of Law
- The honor of the award named for her for the best written brief at the annual Manfred Lachs Space Law Moot Court Competition of the IISL
- Honorary Fellow of the American Institute of Aeronautics and Astronautics (AIAA), the highest rank to which a person can be elected in AIAA and the first woman so recognized, 2005
- IISL Lifetime Achievement Award, 1989
- Women in Aerospace Lifetime Achievement Award (she was the first recipient of this award), 1987
- Fellow of the American Astronautical Society, 1986
- International Academy of Astronautics Theodore von Karman Award, 1986
- IISL Andrew G. Haley Gold Medal, 1968.

Selected Bibliography

Eilene wrote prolifically throughout her career. A very selected list of some of her most notable publications about space law and international cooperation in space follows. The list is in reverse chronological order and divided between reports she prepared for Congress and other reports and articles. A more extensive list of her congressional and non-congressional writings through 1992 is available in Nandasiri Jasentuliyana's edited book *Space Law: Development and Scope.*[33] An inclusive list of all of her non-congressional publications through her death in 2009 is available on the Internet.[34] In addition, her papers are in two archives, one at the National Air & Space Museum and the other at the University of Mississippi.

1. *Key Congressional Publications*

1. U.S. Congress. Senate. Committee on Commerce, Science and Transportation. Introduction. In: Space Law and Related Documents. 101st Congress, 2nd Session. S. Print. 101-98. Washington, U.S. Government Printing Office, June 1990.

2. U.S. Congress. Senate. Committee on Commerce, Science and Transportation. Space Law: Selected Basic Documents. Second Edition. 95th Congress, 2nd session. Washington, U.S. Government Printing Office, December 1978.

3. U.S. Congress. Senate. Committee on Aeronautical and Space Sciences. International Cooperation in Space: A Symposium. 92nd Congress, 1st Session. Document No. 92-57. Washington, U.S. Government Printing Office, December 1971.

4. U.S. Congress. Senate. Committee on Aeronautical and Space Sciences. International Cooperation and Organization for Outer Space. 89th Congress, 1st Session. Doc. 55. Washington, U.S. Government Printing Office, August 12, 1965.

33 *Id.* at 257-261.

34 The list is available at the following websites: www.SpacePolicyOnline.com, http://www.iislweb.org/docs/Writings_of_Eilene_M_Galloway.pdf and www.spacelaw.olemiss.edu.

5. U.S. Congress. Senate. Committee on Aeronautical and Space Sciences. United States International Space Programs: Texts of Executive Agreements, Memoranda of Understanding, and Other International Arrangements, 1959-1965. Doc. 44. Washington, U.S. Government Printing Office. July 30, 1965.

6. U.S. Congress. Senate. Committee on Aeronautical and Space Sciences. Documents on International Aspects of the Exploration and Use of Outer Space, 1954-1962. Staff Report. 88th Congress, 1st session. Doc. 18. Washington, U.S. Government Printing Office, May 9, 1963.

7. U.S. Congress. Senate. Committee on Aeronautical and Space Sciences. Legal Problems of Space Exploration: A Symposium. 87th Congress, 1st session. Doc. 26. Washington, DC, U.S. Government Printing Office, March 22, 1961.

8. U. S. Congress. Senate. Special Committee on Space and Aeronautics. Space Law: A Symposium. 85th Congress, 2nd session. Washington, DC, U.S. Government Printing Office, December 31, 1958.

9. U.S. Congress. Senate. Committee on Armed Services. Guided Missiles in Foreign Countries. Committee Print. Washington, D.C. U.S. Government Printing Office. April, 1957.

2. *Key Non-Congressional Publications*

1. Space Law for the Moon/Mars Mission. Space News, March 30, 2009, 33.

2. Sputnik and the Creation of NASA: A Personal Perspective. In: NASA's 50 Years of Exploration and Discovery. NASA, Washington, D.C., 2008. 48-49.

3. Maintaining International Space Cooperation for Peaceful Uses. Journal of Space Law, vol. 30, no. 2, Fall 2004, 311-315.

4. Law for Space Activities in the 21st Century. In: Air and Space Law in the 21st Century, eds. Marietta Benkö and Walter Kröll. Institute of Air and Space Law the University of Cologne, Germany. 2001. (Liber Amicorum for Karl-Heinz Böckstiegel), 326-338.

5. Existing UN Space Treaties: Strengths and Issues. United Nations Conference on the Exploration and Peaceful Uses of Outer Space (UNISPACE III). Workshop on Space Law in the 21st Century. Vienna, Austria. Session 1. July 20, 1999. 8 pp.

6. NASA at 40: What Kind of Space Agency Does America Need for the 21st Century? Testimony before the U.S. House of Representatives Committee on Science, Subcommittee on Space and Aeronautics. October 1, 1998.

7. Space Law in the 21st Century. Journal of Space Law, vol. 26, no. 2, 1998. 187-192.

8. Guidelines for the Review and Formulation of Outer Space Treaties. 41st Colloquium on the Law of Outer Space. Melbourne. Australia, October 1998. IISL-98-IISL.4.01. 245-253.

9. Organizing the United States Government for Outer Space: 1957-1958. Presented at Reconsidering Sputnik: Forty Years Since the Soviet Sputnik. Symposium sponsored by NASA Office of Policy and Plans/History Office, National Air and Space Museum, George Washington University Space Policy Institute, Kennan Institute for Advanced Russian Studies. September 30 – October 1, 1997, Washington, DC.

10. International Lunar Workshop: Towards a World Strategy for the Exploration and Utilization of Our Natural Satellite. European Space Agency, Beatenberg, Switzerland, 31 May – 3 June 1994. Discussion Paper for Working Group 3: Political, Legal and Economic Aspects of a Return to the Moon.

11. Legal and Regulatory Framework for Solar Power Satellites. In: Glaser, Peter et al, eds. Solar Power Satellites: the Emerging Energy Option. Ellis Horwood, New York, 1993. 183-197.

12. Creating Space Law. In: Jasentuliyana, Nandasiri ed. Space Law: Development and Scope. Westport CT and London, Praeger, 1992. 230-256.

13. Law, Science, and Technology for the Moon/Mars Missions. 33rd Colloquium on the Law of Outer Space, Dresden, Germany, October 5-13, 1990. 195-205. IISL-89-081.

14. International Institutions to Ensure Peaceful Uses of Outer Space. Symposium on Conditions Essential for Maintaining Outer Space for Peaceful Purposes organized by the International Institute of Space Law and the United Nations University in Cooperation with the Peace Palace and the Hague Carnegie Foundation, the Hague, Netherlands, March 12-13, 1984. Published in Annals of Air and Space Law, vol. IX, 1984, 303-327.

15. Law and Security in Outer Space: The Role of Congress in Space Law and Policy. Journal of Space Law, vol. 11, No. 1 & 2, Spring & Fall 1983, 35-50.

16. Perspectives for Further Development of Space Law Pertaining to the Settlement of Disputes. International Colloquium on the Settlement of Space Law Disputes organized by the Institute of Air and Space Law of the University of Cologne in cooperation with the Space Law Committee of the International Law Association, the International Institute of Space Law, and the German Society for Aeronautics and Astronautics, Munich, Germany, September 13-14, 1979. Published in: Settlement of Space Law Disputes, Karl-Heinz Böcksteigel, ed. (1980).

17. The United States Congress and Space Law. Annals of Air and Space Law, vol. 3, 1978, 395-407.

18. Statement to the Legal Subcommittee of the United Nations Committee on Peaceful Uses of Outer Space as Observer of the International Astronautical Federation, March 1977.

19. Consensus as a Basis for International Space Cooperation. 20th Colloquium on the Law of Outer Space. Prague, Czechoslovakia, 1977, 105-111.

20. Applicability of Space Treaties to the Uses of Outer Space. Annals of Air and Space Law, vol. 1, 1976, 205-212.

21. Perspectives for Analyzing Legal Implications of Outer Space Problems. Symposium on Man's Landing on the Moon: Legal Implications and Perspectives, University of Mississippi School of Law, April 10, 1969.

22. Congress and Outer Space: 1957-1958. Conference on Impact of Aerospace Science and Technology on Law and Government, sponsored by the American Institute of Aeronautics and Astronautics and the American Bar Association, Washington, D.C., August 28-30, 1968.

23. The United Nations Ad Hoc Committee on the Peaceful Uses of Outer Space: Accomplishments and Implications for Legal Problems. 2nd Colloquium on the Law of Outer Space, London, United Kingdom, 1959. 30-41.

24. The Community of Law and Science. 1st Colloquium on the Law of Outer Space, the Hague, the Netherlands, 1958. 59-62.

Chapter IX **Rolando Quadri** (22.12.1907 – 2.4.1976)

Sergio Marchisio*

A. The Scientific Personality

Rolando Quadri was one of the most original and somehow genial Italian international lawyers. His personality was characterized by an equally remarkable capacity to generate ideas and to produce an impressive quantity of work. The scientific activity of *Quadri* can be divided in two periods. During the first (1932-1954), which coincided with his teaching of international law at the University of Padua, he showed a strong interest for some specific aspects of international law, to which he consecrated several monographs, such as those concerning the subjection in international law, the legal condition of private ships and the jurisdiction over foreign States. In these works he started the elaboration of a methodology which was presented as a sort of fair half way between the abstract formalism of the continental European schools of law and the excessive pragmatism of the Anglo-Saxon systems. His statement aimed at conciliating the adherence to the legal experience with the need for a systematization of the data deduced from the interpretation of that experience so as to find an inherent harmony within the observed legal system.

His interest for space law belongs to a period when he was mainly concentrated on the pursuit of a broader theoretical design, where law was considered synonymous with power, even in a society, such as the international, where a central authority defected. In a more general perspective, it is worthy

* Full Professor of International Law at the University Sapienza of Rome.

Stephan Hobe (ed.), Pioneers of Space Law
© 2013 *International Institute of Space Law.* ISBN *978-90-04-24027-8. pp. 151-165*

of note that *Quadri* envisaged the foundation of international law in the balance among the dominant forces of the international society, which tended to give a certain shape to such community. Law indeed was for *Quadri* the product of the leading forces that in the international society impose their collective will over the States considered *uti singuli*. Such an approach would necessarily lead to privilege the criterion of effectiveness in assessing the legal consequences of the behaviour of States. Of particular interest for the matter of outer space activities' regulation was the theory of *Quadri* on the foundation of the power of the flag's State over the private ship of its nationality. General international law considered the effective connection between a certain community or activity and a State in order to attribute to the State itself jurisdiction over that community or activity when it was detached in territory *nullius* or, per analogy, in spaces beyond national jurisdictions.

The second phase of *Quadri's* scientific production, starting from 1954 and lasting until 1970, coincided with his teaching at the Faculty of Law of the University of Naples and was marked by his major contributions to the general theory of international law, both public and private.[1] Worthy of note are for instance the contributions in the field of private international law, where he elaborated the unilateralist function's theory of the conflict of laws rules. In this sense, *Quadri* was a "generalist", showing equal interest for all aspects of international law in a time when the tendency towards a greater specialization was still unknown among the writers of international law. Since the second war, *Quadri* treated in several monographic works many themes of public international law, including international cosmic navigation. In 1959 he wrote in Italian a work titled "*Prolegomeni di diritto cosmico*"[2] and in the same year he gave in French his second course at the Hague Academy of International Law, the title of which was "*Droit international cosmique*".[3]

1 *See* Benedetto Conforti, *L'opera di Rolando Quadri*, Rivista di diritto internazionale, 5-27 (1978).

2 Rolando Quadri, *Prolegomeni di diritto cosmico*, I Diritto internazionale, 260 *et seq.* (1959).

3 It followed the first course done in 1952 on "The Foundations of Legal Force of International Law" and preceded the third "Cours général de droit international public" delivered in 1964. *See* Rolando Quadri, *Droit international cosmique*, *in* III Recueil des cours de l'Académie de droit international de la Haye, 505 *et seq.* (1959).

Thus he can legitimately be included in the restricted group of lawyers that were at the root of space law and are indeed to be designated as "pioneers" of that discipline. He contributed in fact to opening new areas of thought, research and development with relation to a sector which was undergoing a profound transformation in the second half of the fifties. These pioneers paved the way by clearing paths, building roads, and digging trenches. In particular, *Quadri* can be envisaged as one of the major tenants of the so-called "functional" approach to outer space law.

B. International Cosmic Law

Quadri was drilled by themes such as "cosmic" law", which he developed in particular with reference to the power of government, territorial sovereignty and its limits, the analogy between maritime and aerial navigation on the one side and cosmic navigation on the other. In the construction of this new branch of law he cared to eliminate every element of a patrimonial character or private law orientation, such as the application of the principle of Roman law *ad inferis usque ad sidera.*[4] As *Benedetto Conforti* recalled, those who were close to him in the years between 1957 and 1959 could remember how much he accentuated, in the study of such a new, if not futuristic, theme, his characteristic enthusiasm and even amusement in the research. In his work about cosmic law he criticized, and ridiculed in its excesses, any "spatial" conception concerning the regulation of cosmic activities, namely any conception aimed at distinguishing the legal regime of the different spaces and at drowning from it the legal or illegal nature of the relative activities.[5] For *Quadri* the fundamental principles of cosmic law should have had a "functional" character in a pure state, because cosmic activities shied away from a control of spatial type similar to that exercised over maritime and aerial navigation. As a consequence, for him cosmic activities were not to be considered licit or illicit because of their localization, but depending on their peculiar characters. From the point of view of the cosmic objects and activities, space was to be considered as a continuous environment, without it being

4 Digeste XLIII, 24, 224.

5 *See* Conforti, *supra* note 1, at 18.

possible to distinguish among atmospheric and extra-atmospheric spaces, between troposphere, or eventually stratosphere, upper zones and so on.

The *quaestio iuris* indeed was not to whom the cosmic space belonged, either to the underneath State or to no State at all, but to ascertain which cosmic activities were permitted and which were prohibited.[6] The conclusion was that, as in the case of radiotelegraphy and of the radio waves, cosmic activities were incoercible, and, as a consequence, they should be considered free unless and until they would become incompatible with or infringe upon the rights of other States.

His interest was concentrated on some issues that we should consider within the times of the first development of space activities when *Quadri* wrote his scientific contributions. In this context, he addressed the state of the art of the discipline and, in particular, of the doctrine of cosmic law. For him, there were no precursors in the proper sense of the word, but traditional theoreticians that tried to apply to the cosmic environment the legal work already done within maritime or aerial law. In this reductive way he evaluated for instance the contribution of *Charles Chaumont*, written in 1958, concerning the problems of international law of the extra-atmospheric space.[7] On the contrary, he found extremely promising, in his "functional" perspective, the hint given by *Schönborn* in 1929, in his course at the Hague Academy of International Law on the legal nature of the State's territory.[8]

In this perspective, *Quadri* was aware of the connection in this field between the technological progress and armament, recalling that towards the end of the Second World War, Germany had been able to launch engines beyond 200 km from the soil of the Earth. After the war new instruments ap-

6 *See* Quadri, *supra* note 2, 298 *et seq.*

7 Charles Chaumont, *Les problèmes du droit international de l'espace extra-atmosphérique*, Institut des hautes études internationales de l'Universite' de Paris, 3 *et seq.* (1958-1959).

8 This author expressed in fact the view that the State's borders in the cosmic space would depend on the advancement of the technique in the broadest sense of the term: "Sa hauteur pourra varier suivant la nature des droits souverains, matériels, éxercés et suivant la technique nécessaire pour les fire valoir". Walther Schoenborn, *La nature juridique du territoire, in* V Recueil des cours de l'Académie de droit international de la Haye, at 158 (1929).

peared, such as the cruising and ballistic missiles capable of being launched at a height of more than 8000 km. He underlined that the legal aspects raised by this kind of arms were practically the same as those posed by the launch of artificial satellites (first of them *Sputnik I*, launched on October 4, 1957 by the U.S.S.R.) and by the activities of cosmic exploration.[9] He recognized, however, as reasons of Cold War why, from 1958 on, issues concerning disarmament were treated separately from those regarding the peaceful uses of outer space. This diplomatic scheme, we should admit, is still in force, seeing on the one side the work of the United Nations Committee on the Peaceful Uses of Outer Space (UNCOPUOS) and the other that of the Commission on Disarmament and of the First Committee of the General Assembly.[10]

C. Functional Spatial Theory

For him the real birth of a veritable doctrine of international cosmic law remounted to the years preceding the first announcements, by the U.S. and the U.S.S.R., in the middle of the fifties, of their intention to launch artificial satellites during the International Geophysical Year. Since then, the doctrine exploded, following arbitrary perspectives and fantasist theories: astronautical law, intersidereal or interplanetary law, interstellar law, or even "meta-law", considered applicable to the relations between human beings and other planetary communities.[11] Furthermore, he noted also that, starting in 1956, some consideration was given to space issues in the general international law works. Reference was made mainly to the work of his compatriot *Mario Giuliano*.[12]

9 Aldo Armando Cocca, *Reflexiones sobre derecho interplanetario*, Revista de derecho internacional y Ciencias diplomaticas, 191 *et seq.* (1958). *See* also John Cobb Cooper, *Legal Problems of Upper Space*, The Journal of Air law and Commerce, 308-316 (1956).

10 *See* Sergio Marchisio, *The Evolutionary Stages of the Legal Subcommittee of the United Nations Committee on the Peaceful Uses of Outer Space (COPUOS)*, 31 Journal of Space Law, 219-242 (2005).

11 John C. Hogan, *Legal Terminology for the Upper Regions of the Atmosphere and for the Space beyond the Atmosphere*, 51 Am. J. Int'l L., 370 *et seq* (1957). For the others authors who dealt with such issues, *see* Quadri, *supra* note 3, 512-514.

12 Mario Giuliano, I diritti e gli obblighi degli Stati 433 and 478 (1956).

But what shocked him mostly was the conservative attitude assumed by the doctrine vis-à-vis such new experiences. Instead of trying to elaborate new categories and concepts, the doctrine relied on the consolidated precedents concerning maritime and aerial navigation, assuming improper analogies between the relative legal regimes. *Quadri* had clearly in mind the theoretical and practical importance of the subject matter, underlining that the topic was of *exceptional* interest to legal scholars. He had also the crystal clear perception that such activities could be carried out for the benefit of the humanity or for its destruction.

His proposal was to assume a functional perspective. It was not the extra-terrestrial localisation of the activities that would have qualified them as "cosmic", since such an approach would have required necessarily the determination of the distance from the Earth from which such qualification could be attributed. However, this problem was never solved, and, in our current perspective, still remains unsolved. Similarly, the criterion of the propulsion appeared to him equally inadmissible, because it would have led to the conclusion that the return of a space object to the Earth was outside the scope of cosmic law. Hence, *Quadri* advocated complete freedom from the spatial approach, stating that there was no need to distinguish between spatial and terrestrial activities. If the objective was to legitimize the autonomy of international cosmic law, it was necessary to get rid of any idea of spatial character. Any activity, as well as any object should be defined as cosmic if its nature was intrinsically cosmic.

As for the terminology, he explained that his preference for "cosmic law" was due to the absence in it of any reference to the spatial dimension. For the same reason he refused also the term "law of outer space", which was to become the most popular in our doctrine, because, once again, for him the relevant element was not the localisation of the activity but its function and nature.

D. The Cosmic Freedoms of States

On the basis of these premises, *Quadri* developed the second part of his conception concerning the nature of the rules of international cosmic law and deepened the positive foundation of the cosmic freedoms of States. If such law was an emerging branch of law, he asked himself which were the positive rules already in force to solve the emerging difficulties. In this line he contested the view expressed by *Eugene Pépin* in his Report to the American Society of International Law of April 25, 1958 in which it was said that there was no legal rule applicable to the circulation of spacecrafts into space and that space penetration and circulation were to be considered free from any regulation.[13] For a consistent part of the doctrine, in other words, law was facing a legal void, apart from the development of "ideas" and "theories".

At the same time, and even more strongly, he opposed the other side of the coin, namely the views according to which aerial law, together with the principles embodied in the Conventions of Paris (1919) and Chicago (1944), should be considered as applicable to the cosmic engines as well as beyond the terrestrial atmosphere. This was, in particular, the opinion expressed by another well known Italian international lawyer, *Riccardo Monaco*, who proposed, arguing *a contrario* from Articles 1 of the Paris and Chicago Conventions which attributed to the State the full and exclusive sovereignty to the limits of the atmosphere, that beyond such atmosphere space should be considered as *a res communis omnium*.[14] This kind of conclusion, perfectly coherent and legitimate, was not in line with the "functional approach" and for that was always underestimated by *Quadri*, who conceived it as a recognition of the vertical limit to the State's sovereignty and the assimilation of cosmic law to aerial law.

Finally, he contested the theories of the *Soviet* author, *Evgeny A. Korovin*, who was inclined to admit that a new law had tacitly formed from the behaviour of the space faring nations and of the States whose rights were affected by such behaviour.[15]

Rather, it was the opinion of *Quadri* that the rules were still in a process of consolidation, so that the legal framework was largely insufficient and uncertain, and the time was not ripe for a general convention. He thought that there was no need for "preventive" law. He agreed that the regulations would be negotiated when the situation demanded and not before. Thus safety regulations would follow, not precede, the projection of man into space, and ques-

13 *See* Proceedings of the American Society of International Law, 232 *et seq.* (1958).

14 Riccardo Monaco, *Sovranità statale e spazio superatmosferico*, Rivista di diritto internazionale, 586 *et seq.* (1958).

15 Quadri, *supra* note 3, at 528.

tions of liability were more likely to be set by precedents as yet unknown than by international agreements in anticipation of crashing satellites.[16] In this perspective, he was somehow right, considering that the first text containing general rules regarding outer space was adopted by the General Assembly of the United Nations in 1963, by Resolution 1962 (XVIII) containing the Declaration of Legal Principles Governing the Activities of States in the Exploration and Use of Outer Space.

Furthermore, he excluded that, with regard to cosmic activities, a role should be attributed to necessity, considered as a source of law in itself. Necessity could also be an element for the application of a norm already formed. The nature of things – *Quadri* said – could not constitute *per se* a source of law, new phenomena requiring new rules and imposing the revision of the existing legal categories.

In this line, the notion of territorial sovereignty was totally unsuitable for space. Once again, he criticized the doctrine of cosmic international law for which the fundamental problem consisted in answering the question whether in a vertical sense sovereignty was limited or not. *Usque ad sidera* meant for him *usque ad absurdum*, because the State was unable to ensure an effective order beyond certain spatial limits. Even the opinions of such authors as *Wilfred Jenks*, who advocated that a vertical limit to the territorial sovereignty derived naturally from the cosmic movements, were for *Quadri*[17] unacceptable. In fact, he did not oppose the reality of astronomic phenomena and the fact that space beyond the atmosphere was not susceptible of appropriation through the projection of some particular sovereignty over a fraction of the terrestrial soil. He contested, however, that such physical elements could be adopted as criteria for spatial delimitation in international law. What *Quadri* censured was to raise elements of a purely natural character to the rank of sources of law.

With regard to the freedoms in outer space, *Quadri's* attention was concentrated, as already noticed, on the analogy, that he retained erroneous, between air and cosmic navigation. For him, it was a relevant point that at

16 He quoted Philip W. Quigg, *Open Skies and Open Space*, 37 Foreign Affairs, at 97 (1958).

17 Wilfred Jenks, *International Law and Activities in Space*, 5 International and Comparative Law Quarterly, at 101 (1956).

the beginning of air navigation many authors thought there was a tendency toward the recognition of the freedom of air space, with distance from the Earth's soil indicated variably, or at least of a right of innocent passage.[18] However, the First World War gave clear evidence that neutral States wanted to keep the war's theatre far away from their skies, claiming their sovereign rights over the atmosphere. This claim was then codified in Articles I of the Paris Convention on Aerial Navigation of October 13, 1919 and of the Chicago Convention on International Civil Aviation of December 7, 1944, which consecrated "formally and without opposition" the principle of sovereignty of each State on the atmospheric space overhanging its territory. Henceforth the configuration of the territory of the State as a space having, by projection, a pyramidal form or as a cone with the head at the centre of the Earth, was largely endorsed by the doctrine. But the problem remained about the base of these geometrical figures. Any proposed solution seemed to be not satisfying, because manifestly excessive, mainly if considered in the light of the principle of effectiveness and of the possibility, for a State, to control the infinity of outer space. In fact, for *Quadri* the mentioned Conventions should have been interpreted as strictly limited to their object, without any possible extension to cosmic navigation. In this sense, *Quadri* opposed the view that Article 8 of the Chicago Convention, stating that pilotless aircraft shall not be flown over the territory of a contracting State without special authorization by that State and in accordance with the terms of such authorization, was applicable also to space objects. In his view, this article gave evidence that the Convention was only applicable to aircraft because the requested measures of control as to obviate danger to civil aircraft, could not be adopted by the contracting State with regard to space objects. In conclusion, the two Conventions left the cosmic problem open, without giving any element in favour of the three possible options with regard to the legal nature of outer space: *res communis omnium*, *res nullius* or extension of the territorial sovereignty of the State until at least a certain vertical limit.

The same criticism was developed by the author with regard to the theory of the tacit agreement between the space-faring States, on the one side, and the non-space-faring nations, on the other.[19] This agreement would have

18 Rolando Quadri, Diritto internazionale pubblico, 685-687 (5th ed. 1968).

19 *See* Quadri, *supra* note 3, 549-550.

been concluded immediately before the launch of the first *Soviet* artificial satellite, as evidenced by the absence of any request for prior authorization and/or any subsequent protest. According to *Quadri*, this theory presupposed that before the agreement such kinds of cosmic experiences were prohibited in international law as contrary to the territorial sovereignty of States. Furthermore, the first cosmic launches were certainly presented by the space faring Nations as *faits accomplis*, without any previous authorization. The silence of the non-space-faring nations and the activities of the Committee for Space Research (COSPAR), while not being a diplomatic conference, were rather in favour of the licit character of the mentioned cosmic experiences.

So what was the lesson to be learned by the practice which developed quickly during those years? For *Quadri*, the main conclusion was that the licit or illicit nature of the cosmic activities could be determined with reference to the pre-existing rules of international law, independently from any criterion of localisation. It was impossible, in his mind, to consider the same activity illicit if carried out in atmospheric space and licit if in outer space. Artificial satellites utilized are in fact also part of the atmosphere. In this sense, the functional approach would have fundamentally supported the freedoms of States with regard to their cosmic activities. If States continued to carry out space programmes, this was why they thought that they were compatible with the principle of the respect of territorial sovereignty, which in the opinion of *Quadri* was to be envisaged as the effective power of a State to govern, protected by international law. As a consequence – and this seems to be a very interesting hint given by *Quadri* with regard to the subsequent legal developments – the State which should be considered as having the right of governing its cosmic activities as well as being responsible for their legal consequences was the launching State. In this sense, he underlined the possible comparison with radiotelegraphy, the experience which for the first time broke the dogma of the impenetrability of territorial sovereignty, due to the incoercible nature of the hertzian waves, bringing the principle of the freedom of the ether within the international law of telecommunications. The same was applicable, in his view, to the cosmic objects, leading to the conclusion that all spaces, atmospheric or not, were open to their free circulation.

E. The Problem of Cosmic Peace

The last part of Quadri's contribution to the emerging doctrine on outer space law in the late nineteen-fifties concerned the cosmic freedom of States and its limit, together with a reflection on the problem of cosmic peace. In his view, in fact, the cosmic freedom of States found its roots not in the analogy with the freedom of the High Seas, but on the general principle of international law according to which everything which is not forbidden is allowed. This was a rule, in his opinion, completing every legal system aimed at protecting behaviours that were not prohibited; thus, this liberty ceased every time that it was in contrast with the rights of other States. The extreme consequence of this vision was that for *Quadri* there would be no violation of international cosmic law in case of a destruction or a contamination of cosmic resources *"car la liberté n'a pas d'objet extérieur"*.[20] This statement is today unacceptable in fact and in law, and shows how much the functional theory, for being too rigid, became incompatible with the evolution of the general situation. Furthermore, the theory of *Quadri* was not sufficiently elaborated in relation to the obligation of due regard and respect for the rights of other States, which he admitted to limit the cosmic freedom of States.

Thus, the logic of *Quadri* was brought to the point that the sole task challenging the lawyer was to ascertain which rules of international law, contained in treaties, were capable of imposing limitations on the cosmic freedom of States. He found these kinds of rules only with regard to the prohibition of the use of force and in particular in Article 51 of the U.N. Charter. This was another very interesting hint, if we consider that there is still some doubt about the applicability of the right of self-defence in outer space. The suggestion of *Quadri* was that the mentioned article prohibited cosmic aggression as well as any other form of aggression; at the same time it allowed individual and collective resistance to the aggression, a resistance that was equally lawful by cosmic means likewise by any other means not prohibited by the law of war.

He also invited not to overestimate the limit imposed by such an article. In his view, the U.N. Charter did not regard the preparation of the means that could lead to the violence and did not solve the problem of disarmament and

20 *Id.* at 570.

of a surprise in an eventual attack. In this sense, the preparations of means for the aggression could be distinguished with difficulty from the preparation of the means to resist an attack.

Thus, cosmic freedoms should be inoffensive in the same sense as all freedoms were according to the U.N. Charter. *Quadri* did not see such character as excluding the cosmic armament. In the absence of a specific rule of international conventional law, theories about the exclusively peaceful, scientific, non-military uses of the cosmos were in his opinion only *de iure condendo* aspirations without positive foundation. In other words, there were no rules at the time excluding the principle of freedom of armaments within the cosmic field. He mentioned the U.S. and the major Western countries' official positions, having approved the draft resolution of October 11, 1957. According to these positions the acceptance of obligations in the matter of armaments should be subordinated to the creation of an adequate system of inspection and verification. Moreover, this is still the position of the U.S. and its allies: no engagements concerning disarmament in space without verifiable mechanisms of control. As for the U.S.S.R., it never divided different aspects of the disarmament, as it sprung from the proposals presented on March 15, 1958, which implied evidently the absence of legal limits on the base of common international law.

Quadri saw, indeed, that there was no coincidence between the practice of States in matters of disarmament and the theories asserting that international law antecedent to the first cosmic experiences prohibited military uses of outer space. Nor was there any tacit agreement undergone on the occasion of the International Geophysical Year in order to legalize some activities (pacific, scientific). If States considered that a special convention was needed to prohibit cosmic military experiences, it was evident that they did not consider them as wrongful. The only possible conclusion was that the issue of the military uses of cosmic space – apart from a defence against aggression – had to be solved in line with the complementary rule that protects any activity not prohibited by a special rule.

In *Quadri's* view it was absurd to leave matters of cosmic activities to a legal monopoly of one State or another aimed at impeding the military uses of cosmic space. One could only think, following our author, of a *de facto* monopoly. Furthermore, in his mind the problem of cosmic disarmament could not be separated from the more general issue of disarmament.

Another aspect touched upon by *Quadri* concerned the absurdity of the concept, in case of war, of cosmic neutrality, because neutrality presupposed the existence of frontiers and the localisation of the measures of force aimed at protecting it.[21] In this sense, cosmic peace was in his mind more than necessary: it was indispensable. This because cosmic war would overwhelm the order on the universal plan.

F. Some Specific Issues

Apart from the general picture, *Quadri* addressed also specific issues regarding the international legal regime of space objects and the responsibility for damage caused by them.

Quadri referred to the discussion among writers on the legal condition of space objects, in particular with regard to the issue of the nature of space objects as *res derelictae* advocated by some authors with reference to space objects outside the technical control of the launching State or, even more general, when outside the atmospheric space. Thus, they were to be considered as *res nullius* by *A. Cocca* and *A. Guarino*.[22] For *Quadri* this was once again an erroneous perspective which derived two problems from the doctrinal incapacity to distinguish: the legal condition of space objects and their ownership in internal law. From the standpoint of international law, in a functionalist perspective, the space object was as relevant in fact as the cosmic actvitity itself, and for that it was covered by the principle of freedom. It was to be considered as the technical instrument through which the launching State could carry out its cosmic activity. For international law it was indifferent if the cosmic activity was carried out by a State or by private persons (of whatever nationality) acting under its control.

Sometimes the doctrine, criticized by *Quadri*, had the tendency to speak about the "nationality" of space objects once again in analogy with aerial and maritime law. It was premature, in his mind, to refer to the concept of nationality because it was *in re ipsa* the attribution of a cosmic activity to the launching State. Space objects, in other words, were to be considered as

21 *See* Rodolfo De Nova, *Guerra e neutralità cosmica, in* Atti del 1° Convegno nazionale di diritto cosmico 51-66 (Ludovico Matteo Bentivoglio ed., 1963).

22 Quadri, *supra* note 3, 584-588.

functionally linked to the activity of the launching State[23]. The protection would finish when the space object ceased its function; however, being the property of someone, international law would protect it as the property of foreign subjects.

Concerning the damage caused by space objects, *Quadri* thought that only the launching State could be envisaged as responsible. As for the foundation of such responsibility he thought that the idea of an objective responsibility was excessive and, in any case, without precedents. Furthermore, it seemed illogical to admit the absolute responsibility of a State even in the presence of the evidence that it took all the necessary measures to avoid damage. He recognized that these conclusions could have seemed highly unsatisfactory and for that he understood the proposals advanced by some authors, such as *Isabella de Rode-Verschoor*, of setting up an International Guarantee Fund administered by the United Nations to pay for damage caused by satellites (except in cases where damage was caused intentionally).[24] To him, the theme, finally, did not seem to be particularly urgent.

Lastly, he tackled the issue of the legal regime of the celestial bodies and cosmic resources. In line with his functional theory, for *Quadri* only the principle of freedom could be applied in relation to such bodies and their resources, unless limited by a specific treaty. Henceforth his conclusion was that States were free to install military bases on them, pollute them or even prejudge their future exploitation.

23 *See* also Katherine M. Gorove, *Delimitation of Outer Space and the Aerospace Object. Where is the Law?*, 28 Journal of Space Law, 11- 27 (2000).

24 Isabelle H. Philepina de Rode-Verschoor, *The Responsibility of States for the Damage Caused by Launched-Space-Bodies*, *in* First Colloqium on the Law of Outer Space, at 103 (1958).

G. Selected Bibliography

Le fondement de la force obligatoire du droit international, in I RECUEIL DES COURS DE L'ACADÉMIE DE DROIT INTERNATIONAL DE LA HAYE, 583 *et seq.* (1952).

PROLEGOMENI AL DIRITTO INTERNAZIONALE COSMICO (1958).

Droit international cosmique, in III RECUEIL DES COURS DE L'ACADÉMIE DE DROIT INTERNATIONAL DE LA HAYE, 509 *et seq.* (1959).

Confini di Stato, IV NOVISSIMO DIGESTO ITALIANO, 28 *et. seq.* (1959).

Cours général de droit international public, in III RECUEIL DES COURS DE L'ACADÉMIE DE DROIT INTERNATIONAL DE LA HAYE, 245 *et. seq.* (1964).

DIRITTO INTERNAZIONALE PUBBLICO (5th ed. 1968).

Chapter X C. Wilfred Jenks (7.3.1909 – 9.10.1973)

Steven Freeland*

A. Introduction

Clarence Wilfred Jenks was born in England on 7 March 1909. He was to dedicate a large part of his professional life to the furtherance of international law and the development of space law. His untimely and premature death from a heart attack on 9 October 1973 at the age of 64, while attending a session of the *Institut de Droit International* on international law in Rome, ended a substantial career spanning many years. He left a lasting legacy for many academics and practitioners of international law, including those engaged in the legal regulation of the exploration and use of outer space.

He was actively engaged in a number of significant developments in various areas of international law and published widely, including some seminal works on space law. A selection of his major works is provided at the end of this chapter, indicating the breadth of his scholarship and the diversity of his expertise in relation to significant issues relating to the purpose, structure and functioning of international legal regulation. In this regard, he was able to bring to his research in space law a wealth of experience and knowledge

* Professor of International Law, University of Western Sydney; Permanent Visiting Professor, iCourts – Center of Excellence for International Courts, Copenhagen; Director of the International Institute of Space Law; Member of the Space Law Committee of the International Law Association; Member of Faculty, London Institute of Space Policy and Law. The author gratefully acknowledges the research assistance provided by Rada Popova and Karan Elliot.

Stephan Hobe (ed.), Pioneers of Space Law
© 2013 International Institute of Space Law. ISBN *978-90-04-24027-8. pp. 167-190*

in other aspects of public international law, international organizations and civil service, which makes his writings all the more practical and relevant.

Moreover, given his broad experience, he displayed the dual characteristics of being both a visionary and a pragmatist, carefully balancing the need for legal regulation with the practical application of law to reality. As Jenks himself described, his work in establishing compliance machinery during his career at the International Labour Organization (see below) was:[1] a synthesis of boldness of conception with caution in execution.

This approach to the development of international law and institutions is also evident in his research and writings in the area of space law, which has provided inspiration for succeeding generations of space law scholars.

B. Education and Academic Pursuits

Although he lost his father when he was only 11 years old and thereafter had to assume a position of responsibility beyond his years within his own family, Jenks demonstrated remarkable energy, intellect and determination in undertaking his formal education; personal traits that would be evident during his entire life.

After local schooling in the state education system in Liverpool, England, he won an open scholarship in 1926 that entitled him to undertake his University studies at Gonville and Caius College at the University of Cambridge. His showed a strong interest in history, law and international relations, which was to shape his future professional career. Apart from excelling in his studies, he was also involved in various extra-curricular activities in his areas of interest, and became treasurer of the British Universities League of Nations Society and chairman of the Cambridge University League of Nations Union, as well as being elected as president of the Cambridge Union in 1930.[2]

In 1928, his essay on international arbitration was adjudged as the winning submission for the Cecil Peace Prize awarded by the Institute of

1 ILO, *Director-General's Office, Former Directors-General*, http://www.ilo.org/public/english/bureau/dgo/staff/formers/jenks.htm (last visited Mar. 12 2012).

2 Elihu Lauterpacht, *Jenks, Clarence Wilfred*, *in* Oxford Dictionary of National Biography, http://www.oxforddnb.com/view/article/37599 (last visited Mar. 21 2012).

International Studies at Geneva. This prize was awarded for outstanding written work in Great Britain and Northern Ireland relating to the maintenance of international peace. He was therefore able to undertake part of his studies in Geneva, which would acquaint him with the city where he would spend the majority of his working life, and where he lies buried. He completed his Cambridge studies in history in 1929 and law in 1931, achieving first class honours in both, and was called to the English bar at Gray's Inn in London in 1936.

During his professional life, Jenks retained links to academic pursuits and educational institutions, subsequently receiving honorary degrees from various Universities in Scotland, India, Korea and South America, an indication of the world-wide renown in which he was held. He also took a number of lecturing positions at the British Academy, Yale University and the University of Georgia, and was a Visiting Professor at The Hague Academy of International Law at various times during the 1950s.

In essence, his remarkable ability to successfully combine a demanding and oftentimes challenging professional career at the senior levels of one of the most significant United Nations agencies, whilst at the same time becoming a prolific and highly respected scholar and writer on international law, was a testament to his many exceptional qualities. As noted, the mix of these two 'careers' made him somewhat unique in the world of international law, allowing him to bring a sense of reality to his opinions, without in any way compromising the legal relevance, integrity and value that they offered.

C. Professional Career at the International Labour Organization

After graduating from Cambridge University, Jenks commenced working in 1931 as a member of the Legal Division for the secretariat of the International Labour Organization (ILO) at its headquarters in Geneva, Switzerland.[3] He would remain associated with the ILO for the remainder of his life (a total of

3 The ILO was established in 1919, and became the first specialized agency of the United Nations in 1946. It is the global body responsible for drawing up and overseeing international labour standards and currently has 181 Member States. It is the only *'tripartite'* United Nations agency, in that it brings together representa-

42 years), rising through the ranks of various senior legal and management positions – Legal Adviser, Assistant Director-General, Deputy Director-General, Principal Director-General – until he was appointed as the 6th Director-General of the ILO as from 1 June 1970,[4] a position he held until his death three years later. He would remain intensely loyal to the ILO and its principles, as demonstrated when he declined the opportunity to be appointed to one of the world's most prestigious chairs of international law, because he considered that his "public duty and international public spirit" required him to continue his work in the practical sphere of human rights.[5]

During his distinguished career at the ILO, Jenks was involved in many high-level issues that would have a lasting legacy not only on the functions of the organization itself, but also much more broadly in the development of the international system, particularly after the conclusion of the Second World War. He was, for example, closely involved with the restatement of the organization's aims and purposes during the 1940s, and was a member of the ILO delegation that attended the San Francisco Conference, which led to the establishment of the United Nations in 1945. He was to play an important advisory role in relation to the structure of the specialized agencies of the United Nations that were established shortly afterwards,[6] including, of course, the ILO itself.

As noted above, he was largely responsible for the development of the organization's compliance mechanisms, and had primary responsibility in his various roles for the ILO's activities with regard to international labour standards and human rights. As such, he played a significant role in the development of most of the eight 'fundamental conventions' concluded by the ILO,[7] having presided as Director-General over the adoption of the 1973 Minimum Age Convention only shortly before his death.

tives of governments, employers and workers to jointly shape policies and programs: ILO website, http://www.ilo.org (last visited Mar. 25 2012).

4 *Supra* note 1.

5 *See* Lauterpacht, *supra* note 2.

6 *Id.*

7 These are the Forced Labour Convention (1930), Freedom of Association and Protection of the Right to Organize Convention (1948), Right to Organize and Collective Bargaining Convention (1949), Equal Remuneration Convention (1951),

Jenks' interest in, and concern for human rights and the 'humanity' of mankind and the 'universality' of law would characterise his research and writings in all spheres of international law, including with respect to space law. He had been an international advisor to the American Law Institute on the drafting of its 'Statement of Essential Human Rights', which was one of the texts that formed the basis of probably the most important international document ever created, the Universal Declaration of Human Rights (UDHR), which was adopted on 10 December 1948 by the United Nations General Assembly. The UDHR represented the first clear formal statement agreed by the world community that specified the fundamental human rights of the individual, an area to which Jenks devoted himself with passion and integrity.

Indeed, in 1969, on the 50th anniversary of its establishment, the ILO was awarded the Nobel Peace Prize for its work in the area of human rights – an honour achieved in no small part due to the work of Clarence Wilfred Jenks.

During his entire professional life, Jenks showed extraordinary energy and capacity. He managed to establish himself with distinction as one of the main figures in the ILO during a period when it was refocussing its internal machinery in order to strengthen compliance with the fundamental principles of the organization. Yet, at the same time he was actively engaged with many other aspects of international law, and became one of the most prominent commentators on international law of his time. As already noted, this included his important pioneering work in the area of space law.

D. Commitment to the Codification of the Fundamental Principles of Space Law

For most people, until Sputnik 1 was launched by the Soviet Union on 4 October 1957, the development of a legal regime for outer space was not a particularly important or pressing matter. Whilst there had been some earlier (largely) academic scholarship regarding the nature and scope of laws that might be relevant and appropriate in relation to the exploration and use of

Abolition of Forced Labour Convention (1957), Discrimination (Employment and Occupation) Convention (1958), Minimum Age Convention (1973), and Worst Forms of Child Labour Convention (1999).

outer space, these had generally been discussed only at a hypothetical level, rather than being directed towards practical legal solutions to the complex questions that would arise.

Jenks, however, was an exception. He had displayed an interest in the legal regulation of outer space from early on and was writing about what he regarded as the fundamental principles of space law even before the launch of Sputnik 1. Already in 1956, Jenks had insisted that the exploration and use of outer space had ceased to be within the realms of imaginative fiction.[8] He had concluded by this time that the space beyond the atmosphere of the Earth must be seen in law not as a *terra nullius*, but rather as a *res extra commercium*, and was therefore incapable of appropriation or any form of acquisition by any State.[9]

In his view, therefore, it was clear that the regulation of space activities was a matter for international law, and there was a need to carefully consider the relevant principles to be applied. It is no surprise that, even before the advent of the 'space age' heralded by the first man-made object launched into Earth orbit, Jenks was already regarded as one of the principal contributors to the literature on space law.[10]

He published an important book *Space Law* in 1965, two years before the first United Nations Space Law Treaty, the 1967 Treaty on Principles Governing the Activities of States in the Exploration and Use of Outer Space, including the Moon and other Celestial Bodies,[11] would be concluded. In doing so, he demonstrated his visionary expertise by producing such a volume at a time when the development of space activities was at a relatively embryonic stage. Yet, he was particularly mindful of the need to develop principles for the international legal regulation of such matters, particularly in view of the rapid development of both the scientific and technical aspects relating to space activities that he envisioned, as well as the possibilities and challenges that this brought with it.

8 C. W. Jenks, *International Law and Activities in Space*, 5 Int'l and Comp. L. Quarterly No. 1, 99, 101 (1956).

9 *Id.*, 103-4.

10 John C. Hogan, *Space Law Bibliography*, 23 J. Air L. and Comm., 317 (1956).

11 610 U.N.T.S. 205 (Outer Space Treaty).

When reviewing Jenks' book shortly after it was published, the distinguished international law commentator J.E.S. Fawcett wrote:[12]

> This is the most comprehensive, penetrating and readable study of space law that has yet appeared in English. Dr Jenks was thinking about these matters even before the first sputnik was launched, and it is remarkable how prescient and well-founded his proposals were, written in 1955.

Jenks played an important institutional role in those early days prior to the codification in the United Nations Space Law Treaties of the fundamental legal principles pertaining to outer space. For example, he was Rapporteur of the 1963 session of the *Institut de Droit International* on "The Legal Regime of Outer Space", at which was passed a resolution that began with a paragraph reflecting Jenks' own "universality" philosophy – which was also an integral part of the vocation of the ILO[13] – regarding international legal regulation:[14]

> *Considering* that the legal regime of the exploration and utilisation of outer space and celestial bodies should be inspired by *a spirit of universality.*

As always, Jenks' vision of what was required by way of legal regulation was balanced against an inherent caution about putting in place legal 'solutions' that would be unrealistic or impractical in the circumstances. In his 1965 book, he describes this need for balance between what might be regarded on the one hand as being 'too imaginative' and, on the other, being 'too timid', as follows:[15]

12 J.E.S. Fawcett, *Book Review, C. Wilfred Jenks, 'Space Law'*, 2 Int'l Rel. No. 12, 849 (1965).

13 *See*, for example, an address by Jenks to the Graduate Institute of International Studies, Geneva, *Universality and Ideology in the ILO*, Oct. 27 1969 (copy with author).

14 *Institut de Droit International*, Session of Brussels – 1963, Sept. 11 1963, preambular paragraph 1 (emphasis added) http://www.idi-iil.org/idiE/resolutionsE/1963_bru_02_en.pdf (last visited Mar. 12 2012).

15 C. Wilfred Jenks, Space Law 178-9 (1965).

> While it is important not to act prematurely in regard to space matters in the absence of fuller knowledge of the probable consequences of various possible courses of action, it is equally necessary to avoid the danger that, by always emphasising the importance of not taking action which might be considered premature, we may forget that developments in space will not wait for us to get our thinking straight about the way in which they should be dealt with and may reach a point at which there is no longer any real possibility of rational control unless effective action is taken without undue delay.

Still, he was a great advocate for the need to codify the legal principles relating to the use and exploration of outer space, at one point even citing the works of great literary writers like Franz Kafka and Eugène Ionesco to support the idea of codification.[16] In this regard, he was very conscious of the importance of States crafting, and then adhering to a practical and clear set of legal rules. The development of Jenks' space law theories stemmed from this overall approach to international law. Indeed, he was firmly of the view that space law must find its foundations in international agreements and treaties, the terms of which were acceptable and accepted by all States.

However, he was sufficiently pragmatic and realistic to temper the typical lawyer's temptation to attempt to be too prescriptive at too early a stage. He believed quite rightly that to restrict space activities to an unacceptably stringent set of rules in its infancy would have the unfortunate effect of:[17]

> imprison[ing] the development of space law in concepts and prejudices derived from an earlier stage in the development of international law in which responsible international lawyers no longer believe.

Nevertheless, Jenks' largely positivist but also instinctively pragmatic view of a universal, integrated body of international law reflected in appropriate formalities was not without its critics.[18] Ultimately, however, the international

16 *Id.* at 313.

17 *Id.* at 315.

18 For example, Myers S. McDougal, an American scholar, differed significantly in his vision of international law as it should advance into the future, including to outer space and beyond. He argued that authoritative decision making should be the

legal fraternity at that time supported the Jenks proposal for the development of space law, hence creating a number of treaties and other written legal instruments; a clear endorsement of Jenks' vision for outer space.

Jenks' vision also stemmed from his great respect for the rule of law, and the need therefore to create a legal framework for international activities – including those in outer space – that was relevant and achievable, even in the face of widely diverging viewpoints on some of the underlying philosophical issues that might exist among the various countries of the world. His firm adherence to principle, respect for the rule of law and the imperative for minimum legal and judicial standards often contrasted with prevailing political interests – yet Jenks never waivered in his opinions about the need to uphold fundamental principles.

For example, Elihu Lauterpacht recalls how Jenks' insistence on the independence of the ILO brought him into conflict with the United States for a period while he was Director-General of the organization, so much so that that country briefly withdrew its support for the organization.[19] Yet, Jenks would not be intimidated, and the United Nations subsequently re-joined the organization. On another occasion, Jenks stood firm and successfully opposed draft proposals by a section of the ILO Conference that would have criticised Israel for alleged breaches of its membership obligations – Jenks reasoned that such an initiative was inappropriate in the absence of prior judicial processes.[20]

As Jenks himself once wrote in the context of describing his work at the ILO, but which is also applicable to the international legal regulation of the exploration and use of outer space for peaceful purposes:[21]

> Wisdom requires us to be somewhat detached from politics, but it sanctions no similar aloofness from respect for due process of law. We must be firm in upholding the principle that the rule of law transcends all ideological differences. The more serious ideological differences are, the more important it becomes that we

primary source of international law: S.G. Sreejith, *Whither International Law, Thither Space Law: A Discipline in Transition*, 38 CALIFORNIA WESTERN INT'L L. J. 331, 350 (2008).

19 *See* Lauterpacht, *supra* note 2.

20 *Id.*

21 *See* Jenks, *supra* note 13.

should deal with them within a common framework of commonly accepted rules of law.

As is well known, the development of the legal regulation of outer space followed the path that Jenks (and others) advocated. Once the United Nations General Assembly had, in 1961, accepted that international law applied to the exploration and use by all States of outer space,[22] the rule of law in this area switched from that of an interested spectator to a full and crucial participant.

As a consequence, in the two decades following the creation of the United Nations Committee on the Peaceful Uses of Outer Space (UNCOPUOS) in 1959,[23] five international treaties relating to the exploration and use of outer space for peaceful purposes were concluded: the Outer Space Treaty, the 1968 Agreement on the Rescue of Astronauts, the Return of Astronauts and the Return of Objects Launched into Outer Space,[24] the 1972 Convention on International Liability for Damage Caused by Space Objects,[25] the 1975 Convention on Registration of Objects Launched into Outer Space,[26] and the

22 *See* United Nations General Assembly Resolution 1721 (XVI) on International Co-operation on the Peaceful Uses of Outer Space (20 December 1961), paragraph 1(a), where the General Assembly commends a number of principles to States 'for their guidance in the exploration and use of outer space', including that:

(a) International law, including the Charter of the United Nations, applies to outer space ad celestial bodies.

Note that Article III Outer Space Treaty provides that international law applies to "activities" in outer space.

23 UNCOPUOS was established by the United Nations General Assembly in 1959, shortly after the launch of Sputnik 1: *See* United Nations General Assembly Resolution 1472 (XIV) on International co-operation in the peaceful uses of outer space (1959). It currently has 70 Members, which, according to UNCOPUOS, means that it is 'one of the largest Committees in the United Nations': http://www.unoosa.org/oosa/en/COPUOS/members.html (last visited Aug. 11 2011).

24 672 U.N.T.S., 119.

25 961 U.N.T.S., 187.

26 1023 U.N.T.S., 15.

1979 Agreement Governing the Activities of States on the Moon and Other Celestial Bodies.[27]

E. Jenks' 'Common Law of Mankind' and Its Application to Space Law

Possessing both faith in the dynamism of international regulation, as well as a tangible sense of creative vision, Jenks increasingly turned his attention after the Second World War towards the creation of an international legal framework that would be reflective of law common to all people. In 1958, he published *The Common Law of Mankind*, an innovative legal work of its time. Building on the concepts of 'commonality' and 'universality' that he had developed in that work, he demonstrated progressive foresight by producing *Space Law* in 1965, a volume so early in the development of space activities that some considered it as being too imaginative to have practical relevance.

In 1965, the same year in which he published his ground-breaking work, Jenks was the Storrs Lecturer at Yale University. During this time, he concluded that there were eight essential elements of international law; principles that he – and many others subsequently – believed had greatly contributed to the effectiveness of international law.[28] These principles for the common law of mankind, further elaborated in his 1969 book *A New World of Law? A Study of the Creative Imagination in International Law*, encompassed:

(1) The unity of mankind;
(2) The immorality of the arbitrary use of force;
(3) The limitation over sovereignty by law;
(4) The impartiality of justice administered by third parties;
(5) The importance of good faith;
(6) The importance of fair dealing;
(7) The significance of mutual aid; and
(8) The respect for human dignity.

Incorporating these elements into the development of the substantive principles of international law, Jenks' vision was of a law and a legal order to govern

27 1363 U.N.T.S., 3 (Moon Agreement).

28 Rafael Domingo, The New Global Law 40 (2010).

all nations, reaching even to outer space, and which incorporated the will of all people. To achieve this, he postulated that the legal systems of all States should be analysed with a view to determining a collective will. This 'will of the community' would form the basis of all international law[29] and, as noted above, would be reflected in general and specific formal agreements such as treaties.

From Jenks' perspective, activities in outer space were a mere extension of humankind's existence on Earth, so that the determination of the relevant principles regulating outer space should be governed by the same 'commonality' process as was applicable to Earth.[30] In adopting this 'global' perspective, Jenks courageously rejected traditional views of international law, replacing them with a structure that would have sufficient breadth and depth to cope with the inevitable and ongoing changes to the prevailing geopolitical situation at any one time.[31] He was of the view that:[32]

> [o]ne of the difficulties of expressing the agreed law clearly and creating confidence in the determination of disagreements by objective decision is that the law can neither anticipate all contingencies nor ever be static.

Clearly, his practical experience in senior management roles within a significant international organization during a long period that was characterized by significant geopolitical change and sometimes even upheaval strongly influenced his view. This insight placed Jenks in a unique position to consider the impending development of space law that would evolve over the following decades in a realistic way, highlighting the undoubted mutual interdependence between law and politics in the field of space activities, as well as the effects of changing human values.

Indeed, demonstrating his unswerving commitment to human rights, he asserted that the new international law must preserve human, social, economic and political rights, as well as civil liberties.[33] He understood the

29 Sreejith, *supra* note 18, at 331, 349.

30 Jenks, *supra* note 15, at 315.

31 Domingo, *supra* note 28, at 39.

32 Jenks, *supra* note 13, at 23.

33 Jenks, *supra* note 15 at 2.

practical realities of change, and thus regarded his version of international law as designed not to govern relations between States, but rather as a way of approaching the law of mankind 'in an early phase of its development'.[34]

F. Jenks' Vision of the Fundamentals of Space Law

As noted above, according to Jenks, the principles of space law should be incorporated into his vision of a common law of mankind, which reflected the in parallel relationship between humankind and the 'environment' of humanity. He conceived that this environment was created largely as a result of scientific and technological advancements. At the same time, he believed that it was important not to be overly rigid in the development of legal regimes to apply to changing times; rather, what was necessary was to maintain a generally flexible and generalist approach to the development of legal regulation, in order to successfully move forward in an age of rapid development and advancing technology. Jenks was keen that developments in the future would not be hamstrung by the 'eagerness of the past'.

Much of Jenks' work and commentary regarding space law is based upon the 1963 Declaration of Legal Principles Governing the Activities of States in the Exploration and Use of Outer Space,[35] the first preambular paragraph of which refers to the 'common interest of all mankind'. This was consistent with his view of the basis of international law, and was thus, according to Jenks, the general principle that should define the scope of solutions to problems raised in regard to space law. He therefore encouraged the common interest of mankind as the guiding light towards resolution of space law's conundrums, as a means and mechanism to facilitate co-operation and development.[36]

This view of the regulation of space activities was further emphasised by the first paragraph of the Space Principles Declaration, which provides that:[37]

34 *Id*, at 14.

35 United Nations General Assembly Resolution 1962 (XVIII) on the Declaration of Legal Principles Governing the Activities of States in the Exploration and Uses of Outer Space (1963), (Space Principles Declaration).

36 Jenks, *supra* note 15, 193-4.

37 *See also* Outer Space Treaty, Article 1.

> the exploration and use of outer space shall be carried on for the benefit and interest of all mankind.

Jenks articulated this characterization of the commonality of international law in general, and space law in particular, as follows:[38]

> Space law, like air law, is not a substantive branch of the law ... It consists of an angle of preoccupation with a wide range of diverse problems rather than a well-defined area demarcated by the substance of the problems which it embraces.

In this way, space law was not to be regarded as separate or separated from other aspects of international legal regulation, and thus there was a strong overarching set of principles that shaped and determined the more specific ideals that would apply to the exploration and use of outer space for peaceful purposes. In other words, according to Jenks, it would be inaccurate to look to an all-embracing 'new' set of principles regarding outer space in isolation, or to attempt to address every conceivable issue that might arise. That would be a futile task and, in any event, would not be reflective of the realities of change generated by the inevitable development and evolution of science and technology.

In his 1968 article 'The New Science and the Law of Nations', Jenks expressed his view on the inevitable interaction and interdependence of science and law in the following way:[39]

> Legal thought can never be divorced from the general intellectual currents of the age.

Interestingly, in 1968, in articulating the importance of the interdependence of law and science, and as a further extension of his commonality principle underlying the development of international legal regulation, Jenks drew upon the concept of the 'common heritage of all mankind' – subsequently in-

38 C. Wilfred Jenks, *Seven Stages in the Development of Space Law*, 11 Proceedings of the Coll. on the L. of Outer Space, 246, 262-3 (1968).

39 C. Wilfred Jenks, *The New Science and the Law of Nations*, 17 Int'l and Comp. L. Quarterly, No. 2, 327, 327 (April 1968).

cluded in the Moon Agreement[40] and also the 1982 Convention on the Law of the Sea.[41] He suggested that 'science' was also the common heritage of mankind, emphasising its contribution to, and impact on the global governance regime that he believed should characterise international law in general, including the principles that were to regulate activities in outer space.

Given both that he believed that his commonality of law should also apply to outer space, as well as his close association with the work of the United Nations and the effectiveness of intergovernmental organizations, Jenks was a firm advocate of the United Nations assuming a lead role in the development of the 'law-making' aspects relating to activities in outer space. Although this viewpoint diverged from traditional public international law doctrine, which prescribed that the United Nations (General Assembly) did not represent a 'source of law',[42] Jenks regarded the *sui generis* nature of outer space, and the unique issues that it raised in terms of regulation, as warranting a non-traditional approach.

He believed that this would also help to foster international co-operation and commonality, which would further encourage the peaceful uses of outer space, as long as the treaties that would result from the United Nations discussions were ratified by those States most involved in the exploration and use of outer space.[43]

In arguing for this particular role for the United Nations, Jenks again demonstrated his visionary approach, reasoning as follows:[44]

> There is now a fleeting opportunity to establish the principle that all activities in space, whether pooled or operated independently by individual nations, are subject to the direct regulatory authority of the United Nations, exercised by an

40 Moon Agreement, *supra* note 27, article 11(1).

41 United Nations Convention on the Law of the Sea, 1833 U.N.T.S. 3, article 136.

42 *See* Statute of the International Court of Justice 1 U.N.T.S. 16, article 38(1). For a discussion of the 'sources' of international law – both 'traditional' and 'non-traditional' – as they apply to the regulation of space activities, *see* Steven Freeland, *For Better or For Worse? The Use of 'Soft Law' within the International Legal Regulation of Outer Space*, XXXVI Annals of Air and Space L., 409-445 (2011).

43 Jenks, *supra* note 15, at 183.

44 C. Wilfred Jenks, The Common Law of Mankind 406-7 (1958).

> appropriate body to be created for the purpose. If the principle is established the details can be evolved at leisure ... Why cannot the United Nations, by action of the General Assembly, collectively assume jurisdiction in space in relation to all its members? Hitherto no State has effectively exercised jurisdiction in space. There would therefore be no interference with any existing jurisdiction. Such an action would be entirely without precedent, but the circumstances are equally unprecedented.

Jenks' clear vision about the ever-changing technological and scientific circumstances that would impact upon the nature of space activities, gave him further insights about the need to properly address the problems posed by such developments. Not only did he raise this in the context of outer space, but it was also highly pertinent to his views about a diverse range of important contemporary issues, such as controls over nuclear energy, environmental pollution, the regime of oceans and the Polar Regions.[45]

Shortly after the conclusion of the Outer Space Treaty, Jenks noted some immediate and practical problems and expressed his concern that the Treaty had already included general principles of major importance but, nevertheless, it was clear that detailed arrangements on the practical applicability were yet to be spelled out. Jenks was cognisant of the limitations of developing a vast new regime of space law in isolation. He believed that existing international law relating to matters such as aircraft and telecommunications were also relevant and must be observed.[46]

Furthermore, he argued that, although they were important, treaties were not the answer to all aspects of space activities – international standards, regulations and recommendations all also had a part to play in the international regulation of this new area of activity. In addition, since science and technology, he believed, played an important role in the development of space activities, it was understood that there were instances and issues where law must give way to science.

One important example of this was the way in which the Outer Space Treaty terms would 'require' specific precautions to be taken against the risk of (forward and back) contamination. In Jenks' view, the best approach here

45 Jenks, *supra* note 15, at 328.

46 *Id.* at 186.

was to avoid cumbersome legal regulation, so that the (scientific) experts could determine the most appropriate methods to be adopted, which may themselves change in view of ongoing scientific research and technological development. He was clear that a balance must be struck, between science, legal restrictions and future freedoms. This would require the articulation of policy and principle, but also allow for the flexibility to adapt to changing circumstances. He expressed this view as follows:[47]

> To attempt to predict the course or rate of further development would be hazardous in the extreme, but we can at least attempt to distinguish some of the broad considerations of policy which will call for continuing attention.

As is well known, several of the issues raised in more general terms in the Outer Space Treaty were elaborated upon in the subsequent United Nations Space Law Treaties, although it is also clear that there remain many areas about which the existent legal regime does not comprehensively deal – and thus does not rigidly constrict – in respect of all of the practical issues that stem from the rapid expansion of space activities brought about by the development of space and technology.

Besides laying out the framework within which the regulation of activities in outer space should be regulated, Jenks did, of course, express opinions regarding particular fundamental aspects of space law. In his written work, particularly in his book *Space Law*, he posed many important questions surrounding the emerging law pertaining to outer space, some of which he proceeded to answer, while others were left open for colleagues to ponder.

On the issue of *where does space begin?*, as Jenks rightly observed, the Space Principles Declaration did not deal with the issue of demarcation of space. Where, indeed, is that invisible line between the Earth's atmosphere and outer space? And does anybody care? It seemed not at the time. According to Jenks' predictions, if and when the need arose for a workable definition of demarcation, the answer should lie, he says in the matter at hand, rather than any generalist application. A (sharp) divergence of views, he noted, was inevitable. The parties involved would undoubtedly seek to manipulate defi-

47 *Id.* at 314.

nitions and boundaries to provide the greatest benefit to their cause (be that freedom of use, national security, or other motives).

With this in mind, the most appropriate solution that Jenks felt he could provide at the time was that outer space would be beyond the stratosphere.[48] As is well known, of course, Jenks was certainly not alone in struggling to be more specific on this question, with the issue of demarcation still somewhat unclear some five decades after first he discussed the matter.

In *Space Law*, Jenks discusses the question of *property rights in space*, particularly the question of the private 'ownership' of the Moon. He noted that the answer involved considerations that represented a significant departure from accepted international law. He affirmed that physical occupation of celestial bodies was not permitted – unlike traditional international law on Earth, which permits acquisition of, and sovereignty over unoccupied territories.[49] Jenks, however, did seem to envision some – quite limited – forms of property right in relation to certain activities in outer space, at least with respect to stations located on a celestial body:[50]

> If property transactions should take place in space it would seem appropriate to regard them as governed by the law with which it has the most substantial connection. If anything in the nature of real property rights at a space station on a celestial body were to be recognised, the law applicable there would presumably govern them ... Any recognition of real property rights beyond the limits of such a station would ... raise a major question of policy concerning the basis of authority to confer or recognise such rights.

However, authors vary in their interpretation of Jenks' meaning on this point. A commentator in the minority of commentators interpreted Jenks' opinions as an acceptance of private appropriation under the terms of the Outer Space

48 *Id.* 190-1.

49 *Id.* at 204. For an analysis of the historical and contemporary views regarding the interpretation of the 'non-appropriation' principle as it applies to the regulation of the exploration and use of outer space for peaceful purposes, *see* Steven Freeland and Ram Jakhu, *Article II* in:, Cologne Commentary on Space Law, Volume I – Outer Space Treaty 44-63 (Stephan Hobe, Bernhard Schmidt-Tedd and Kai-Uwe Schrogl 2009)..

50 *Id.*, Jenks at 297.

Treaty. The majority, however, interpreted the Outer Space Treaty as implicitly extending to all parties, including private entities. Interestingly, proponents of this hypothesis often quote Jenks in support of that interpretation:[51]

> States bear international responsibility for national activities in space; it follows that what is forbidden to a State is not permitted to a chartered company created by a State or to one of its nationals acting as a private adventurer.

Related to the issue of property rights and the acquisition of 'territory', Jenks also suggested that the issue of the *use of the natural resources* of outer space and celestial bodies should be regarded as an 'immediate' problem to be addressed. He again argued that, preferably, the appropriate organization to develop and regulate the proper regime was the United Nations. If that were not possible, Jenks suggested that analogies with the situation in Antarctica and the partitioning in Africa regarding the acquisition of territory might be appropriate.[52]

One should always bear in mind that Jenks was contributing his thoughts regarding international law and how it applied to activities in outer space at a time when the two major super-powers – the United States and the Soviet Union – were at the centre of world affairs. This created a culture of 'haves' and 'have-nots', which was not only relevant to Jenks' insights regarding the impact of politics, but also offended his deep sense of humanity and the 'human spirit'.

He recognised that, on the one hand, the two super-powers (with their unique space capabilities) believed that they were entitled to exclude other nations from outer space, whilst, on the other, those countries without space technology or capabilitywere equally strident in their view that they had a right to an allocation of space resources (benefits), despite their (then) current lack of active participation.[53]

51 *Id.* at 201.

52 Jenks, *supra* note 8, 110-1.

53 Sreejith, *supra* note 18, 331, 336.

Jenks understood that it was therefore only natural that lawyers should become involved, even though, in his opinion, they appeared somewhat unhurried in their development of concrete declarations. As he describes it:[54]

> International lawyers have not been slow to explore the challenge which the new scientific and technological developments present for the law, but their collective thinking on the subject is necessarily in a tentative stage of development.

G. Jenks' Legacy – A True 'Pioneer' of International (Space) Law

Clarence Wilfred Jenks was one of the visionaries of the 20th Century, who contributed to the development of international law in a way that very few others have managed to do. Not only was this because of his intense intellect and outstanding professional career and expertise, but also because his work displayed true foresight. He understood the importance, where appropriate, of 'anticipatory action' in areas such requiring regulation in changing circumstances, including with respect to the development of the law of outer space. Already in 1956, he had argued that:[55]

> While it is healthy that the evolution of law should follow rather than anticipate that of life, there are circumstances in which the possibility of developing the law on sound principles depends primarily on an initiative being taken in the matter before de facto situations have crystallized too far.

His contributions to the development of international law in general, as well as the law of outer space in particular, showed a unique mix of foresight, practical and political nuance, progressive ideas, positivism, pragmatism, and an understanding of the possibilities offered by science and technology. This contributed to the fact that much of his work, articulated 60-70 years ago, is still as insightful and relevant today as it was at the beginning of humankind's adventures in outer space. The current pace of technical and scientific development, and the sheer range and extent of space activities, which has

54 C. Wilfred Jenks, *The International Control of Outer Space*, 3 Proceedings of the Coll. on the L. of Outer Space, 3, (1960).

55 Jenks, *supra* note 8, 99, 101.

led to an increase in the number and the type of space actors, is a vindication of Jenks' prescient words in the 1950s; that the regulation of space was, and today continues to be an important matter, with pressing needs for effective rules that not only reflect and note existing problems, but represent much more – indeed, they are rules that anticipate the evolution of life.[56]

Undoubtedly, Jenks contributed to the development of space law not only in the age of its genesis. His ability to see not only the existing issues, but also those that some might have considered as imaginative and not important then, proved to be far-sighted from a contemporary perspective. Jenks is indeed one of the pioneers of space law, who managed to foresee the fast development of space activities and recognized the importance of elaborating an effective and more detailed framework based on the existing international treaties – a need that continues to be on the agenda of space forums today.

In this regard, it is therefore fitting to conclude this brief description of the life and achievements of Clarence Wilfred Jenks, an inspiring pioneer to us all, with his own words all those years ago – words that still represent important truths for all of those concerned with the ongoing development of space law for peaceful purposes:[57]

> It is of paramount importance that the future development of space law should be shaped and moulded by a continuing partnership of bold statesmanship, imaginative legal vision, and thorough grasp of scientific and technological factors involved.

56 *Id.* at 101.

57 Jenks, *supra* note 15, at 313.

Selected Bibliography

Books and papers

The Headquarters of International Institutions: A Study of their Location and Status (Post-war problems) (1945)

The International Protection of Trade Union Freedom (1957)

The Common Law of Mankind (1958)

Human Rights and International Labour Standards (1960)

International Immunities: Law of International Institutions (1961)

The Proper Law of International Organizations (1962)

International Law in a Changing World (1963)

The Prospects of International Adjudication (1964)

Law, Freedom and Welfare (1965) (with A. Larson)

Space Law (1965)

Law in the World Community (1968)

The World beyond the Charter in Historical Perspective: A Tentative Synthesis of Four Stages of World Organization (1969)

A New World of Law? A Study of the Creative Imagination in International Law (1969)

Articles

'The Proposed Peace Act' *Transactions of the Grotius Society,* Vol. 21, Problems of Peace and War, Papers Read before the Society in the Year 1935 (1935) 1-21

'The Maintenance of Migrants' Pension Rights Convention' *Political Science Quarterly,* Vol. 51, No. 2 (June 1936) 215-229

'Nationality, the Flag and Registration as Criteria for Demarcating the Scope of Maritime Conventions' *Journal of Comparative Legislation and International Law,* Third Series, Vol. 19, No. 4 (1937) 245-252

'The International Labour Organization as a Subject of Study for International Lawyers' *Journal of Comparative Legislation and International Law,* Third Series, Vol. 22, No. 1 (1940) 36-56

'The Significance Today of Lorimer's "Ultimate Problem of International Jurisprudence"' *Transactions of the Grotius Society,* Vol. 26, Problems of Peace and War, Papers Read before the Society in the Year 1940 (1940) 35-65

'Regionalism in International Judicial Organization' *The American Journal of International Law,* Vol. 37, No. 2 (April 1943) 314-320

'The Need for an International Legislative Drafting Bureau' *The American Journal of International Law,*Vol. 39, No. 2 (April 1945) 163-179

'The Five Economic and Social Rights' in: *Annals of the American Academy of Political and Social Science,* Vol. 243, Essential Human Rights (January 1946) 40-46

'The Status of International Organisations in Relation to the International Court of Justice' *Transactions of the Grotius Society* Vol. 32, Problems of Public and Private International Law, Transactions for the Year 1946 (1946) 1-41

'The Impact of International Organisations on Public and Private International Law' *Transactions of the Grotius Society,* Vol. 37, Problems of Public and Private International Law, Transactions for the Year 1951 (1951) 23-60

'International Law and Activities in Space' *The International and Comparative Law Quarterly*, Vol. 5, No. 1 (January 1956) 99-114

'Craftsmanship in International Law' *The American Journal of International Law*, Vol. 50, No. 1 (January 1956) 32-60

'An International Regime for Antarctica?' *International Affairs* (*Royal Institute of International Affairs 1944-*),Vol. 32, No. 4 (October 1956) 414-426

'The International Control of Outer Space' *Proceedings of the Colloquium on the Law of Outer Space*, Vol. 3 (1960) 3

'Due Process of Law in International Organizations'*International Organization,* Vol. 19, No. 2 (Spring 1965) 163-176

'The New Science and the Law of Nations' *The International and Comparative Law Quarterly*, Vol. 17, No. 2 (April 1968) 327-345

'Seven Stages in the Development of Space Law' 11 *Proceedings of the Colloquium on the Law of Outer Space*, Vol. 11 (1968) 246

'Democracy and Economic Growth: The Role of the I.L.O.'*The Journal of Modern African Studies*,Vol. 8, No. 2 (July 1970) 293-296

'Realism and Magnanimity in the Law of Nations' *The American Journal of International Law*,Vol. 66, No. 4 (September 1972) 314-323

Chapter XI **Manfred Lachs** (21.4.1914 – 4.1.1993)

Francis Lyall*

No less than four obituaries of Manfred Lachs were carried in 1993 in the eighty-seventh volume of the American Journal of International Law. That and they are testimony to the high regard in which he was held, to the extent of his influence, and to his engaging personality.[1] Aided by fluency in five languages Manfred Lachs was a good communicator, persuasive and far-seeing. While this chapter celebrates him as a pioneer of space law, his contribution to the development of international law extended across all its elements. Lachs was, of course, of major importance in the initial stages of space law, particularly in his less documented role within COPUOS, but that was within the wider context of his general philosophy. That philosophy may be clearly seen in the after-mentioned General Course he delivered at The Hague Academy of International Law in 1980,[2] a set of fifteen lectures that is

* Emeritus Professor of Public Law, University of Aberdeen, Scotland, U.K.

1 *In Memoriam: Judge Manfred Lachs (1914-1993)*, 87 Am. J. Int'l. L. 414-23 (1993): Oscar Schachter, *The UN Years: Lachs the Diplomat*, 414-6; Stephen M. Schwebel, *On the Bench: Lachs the Judge*, 416-9; Thomas M. Franck, *The Private Lachs: Life as Art*, 419-20; Sudhir K. Chopra, *The Teacher: Lachs at the Hague Academy*, 420-23. See also I.P.H. Diederiks-Verschoor, *Judge Manfred Lachs: An Obituary*, 22 *J. Space Law* 1-3 (1994); R. Higgins, *Manfred Lachs*, The Independent (U.K.), Feb. 16, 1993.

2 Manfred Lachs, The Development and General Trends of International Law in Our Time, General Course on Public International Law, The Hague Academy of International Law, 169 1980-IV *Receuil des Cours*, 9-337.

Stephan Hobe (ed.), Pioneers of Space Law

ISBN 978-90-04-24027-8. pp. 193-210

a *tour de force*. Although Lachs himself was formed by western and socialist legal and political communities, he there shows an impressive sweep of historical understanding drawn from a rich variety of sources.

In the Twentieth century law had to cope with a new ordering of international society. From the mid-1800s scientific understanding had increased. New technologies were invented. Older technologies were improved. In the twentieth century the spur of two world wars and international rivalries were not irrelevant in technological advance. In 1957 Sputnik I was launched. International law had to respond to all these developments. The contribution of Manfred Lachs was significant. He understood that rules are necessary, but that they had to be adaptable to change as circumstances altered. If necessary, rules had to be invented. In his words:

> Law is a vital and necessary part of the daily affairs of nations: trains cross borders, planes leave airfields and land in remote countries, ships sail under many flags, States trade with one another, and people travel to foreign lands, make overseas telephone calls, send letters around the globe, and tune in to radio and television broadcasts beamed from foreign stations. All this is law. Without these routine events would be impossible. International law though imperfect and inadequately developed in some respects, is thus more than an abstract theory honored in the breach: instead it plays an important role in the daily lives of nations and individuals alike.[3]

However, the first half of the Twentieth century fumbled the task. The First World War saw the demise of two empires but the first attempt at a true world organisation, the League of Nations proved unsatisfactory in concept and application. The Second World War made second thoughts necessary and a new response to the emergent problems of those "daily lives of nations". The League was replaced by the United Nations and the UN family of international agencies was created. The International Court of Justice replaced the Permanent Court of International Justice. Manfred Lachs figured in that new response because of his clarity of thought and his flair for moulding agree-

3 Manfred Lachs, *Some Reflections on the Contribution of the International Court of Justice to the Development of International Law*, 10 Syracuse J. Int'l L. & Com. 239-78 (1983).

ment. He understood that under modern conditions international principles had to be set and developed into binding law more swiftly than had been the case hitherto. In particular for our purposes here his role in the early discussions as to the content of space law was crucial. He clearly saw the need for new rules to be swiftly agreed with as great a general acceptance as possible. In this he succeeded, and it may here be noted that his role in securing that agreement was taken up only some fifteen years after his entry into the UN world.

The closing years of the Second World War saw the emergence of Manfred Lachs on the world scene. Born the son of a lawyer on 21 April 1914 in Stanislau (now Ivano-Frankivsk in western Ukraine), Lachs graduated in Law (LL.M. and LL.D.) from the Jagellonian University, Cracow, in 1937. Thereafter he studied at the University of Vienna and in 1939 gained a doctorate from the University of Nancy. When the Second World War broke out he was in the United Kingdom at the London School of Economics and Cambridge University. As a result he survived, while back on the continent his entire family was wiped out in the Holocaust.

During the Second World War Lachs was a member of the Polish forces and served the Polish Government in Exile both as a legal adviser and as a member of the Polish National Council. He was part of the delegation accredited by Polish Government in Exile to the UN War Crimes Commission (1944). Not unconnectedly he published two articles on war crimes,[4] a book following soon after.[5] Shortly afterwards he was part of the Nuremberg prosecution of Nazi crimes committed in Poland. However, he did not remain in the West, deciding to return to Poland where he became one of the few returnees from the West to attain a high position. He served as Director of the Legal and Treaties Department of the Polish Ministry of Foreign Affairs, 1947-60, as Legal Adviser to the Minister of Foreign Affairs of Poland, 1960-66, and as Director of the Institute of Legal Sciences of the Polish Academy of Sciences, 1961-67. During this time he was also a much-appreciated Professor in the

4 Manfred Lachs, *War Crimes – Political Offences*, 56 Jur. Rev. 27-41 (1944); cf. M. Lachs, *The Unwritten Laws of Warfare*, 20 Tulane L. Rev. 120-128 (1945).

5 Manfred Lachs, War Crimes: An Attempt to Define the Issues, (1945).

Academy of Political Science, Warsaw, 1949-52, lecturing in international law at Warsaw University and writing numerous articles, mainly in Polish.[6]

Lachs was called on to serve the Communist government internationally, most obviously at the UN, attending the Preparatory Commission in London, 1945, and thereafter as part of the Polish delegation to twenty sessions of the General Assembly. The redoubtable Oscar Schachter, who as sometime Director of the General Legal Department and legal adviser to the UN and successive Secretaries-General was well-placed to comment, specifically notes that Lachs' adherence to official policy was absolute, irrespective of what his personal views might have been.[7] Notwithstanding, Lachs was popular and well-regarded in UN circles, being known as a skilled international lawyer rather than a spokesman for Communism. He was soon elected to the Sixth Committee (Legal) of the General Assembly, and as its Chairman on three occasions (1949, 1951 and 1955). Given his historical involvement in the prosecution of war crimes it is not surprising that in the Sixth Committee he worked on what became the Genocide Convention.[8] Elected in 1962 to the International Law Commission he was active in its consideration of the Law of Treaties,[9] and in the initial discussions of state succession where he was influential in setting out the broad principles of the law. In other areas Lachs was the Polish representative in the negotiation of what became the 1968 Treaty on the Non-Proliferation of Nuclear Weapons.[10]

6 Cf. MANFRED LACHS, THE POLISH-GERMAN FRONTIER: LAW, LIFE AND LOGIC OF HISTORY, (1964).

7 O. Schachter, above n. 1, at 415.

8 Convention on the Prevention and Punishment of the Crime of Genocide, Paris, December 9, 1948, 78 U.N.T.S. 277 (1948). Lachs may have been responsible for Poland's reservation of non-acceptance of Art. XII, it "considering that the Convention should apply to Non-Self-Governing Territories, including Trust Territories". Art. XII permits but does not require contracting parties to extend the application of the Convention to all or any territories for the conduct of whose foreign relations it is responsible.

9 Convention on the Law of Treaties, Vienna, May 23, 1969, 1155 U.N.T.S. 331 (1969); 8 I.L.M. 679 (1969).

10 Treaty on the Non-Proliferation of Nuclear Weapons, London, Moscow, Washington, July 1, 1968, 729 U.N.T.S. 161 (1968); 7 I.L.M. 809 (1968). Lachs had been one of

His judicial career began with membership of the UNESCO Arbitral Tribunal in 1949 and of the Permanent Court of Arbitration in 1956. In 1966 he was elected a member of the International Court of Justice by majorities unprecedented in both the Security Council and General Assembly and took up office in February 1967. He was re-elected to the Court in 1975 and 1984 by similar majorities, on both occasions securing nominations from a very wide spread of legal traditions. He served as President of the Court from 1973 to 1976, surprisingly early in his career on the Court and a clear recognition of his qualities. So far the longest serving judge of the International Court, he died in office on 14 January 1993.

When Lachs took his seat the International Court of Justice was not widely esteemed, attitudes to the decision in the South-West Africa (Second Phase) Case being symptomatic.[11] Socialist countries abhorred the notion of third party adjudication of international disputes, and Third World countries distrusted what they perceived as a bias towards Western interests. Throughout his tenure Lachs was one whose pragmatism helped restore the Court's reputation, making more secure its role in international affairs as the principal international judicial organ, in its relations with other UN organs, and to a degree as the constitutional court of the UN system.[12] He introduced the practice of the ICJ making an annual report to the UN General Assembly, and frequently attended its sessions. He made the ICJ part of The Netherlands diplomatic and social scene, an effort that partially explains why The Hague has become the seat of a number of international tribunals. Serving for more than two decades as Chairman of the ICJ Rules Committee, and concerned that recourse to the Court should not be unnecessarily discouraged, he was responsible for major changes to the Rules that made its processes more user-friendly. During his time he took part in most of the cases and the court de-

the authors of a precursor of the 1968 Treaty, the Rapacki Plan, a Polish proposal to establish a nuclear-free zone in Europe made to the 1957 UN General Assembly.

11 South West Africa Cases (Ethiopia v. South Africa; Liberia v. South Africa) Second Phase, Judgement, 1966 I.C.J. 6 (July 18).

12 Edward McWhinney, Judge Manfred Lachs and Judicial Law-making: Opinions on the International Court of Justice, 1967-1993 1-115 (1995); L.V. Prott, *The Judicial Philosophy of Manfred Lachs in* Essays in International Law in Honour of Judge Manfred Lachs 423-447 (Jerzy Makarczyk, ed., 1984).

cisions that were made. Some did consider him perhaps too willing to have regard to diplomatic or political elements in cases,[13] but he was sensitive to any suggestion that his background played any role in his decisions.[14] In only two instances did he deliver a dissenting Opinion.[15] His Separate Opinions and Declarations were few. These, often by way of a procedural comment, usually usefully gloss the majority judgements to which they were attached.[16] As McWhinney notes, on occasion a Separate Opinion by Lachs could easily be converted into a dissent, but, in the higher interest of ending litigation through the final resolution of disputes, Lachs preferred to respect Court

13 *See Conversations with Sir Eli Lauterpacht, 6th interview by L. Dingle*, http://www.dspace.cam.ac.uk/handle/1810/197071, citing the Nuclear Test cases, Australia v. France, 1974 I.C.J. 253 (December 20) and New Zealand v. France, 1974 I.C.J. 457 (December 20), in which the Court declared it unnecessary to make a decision on the legalities following upon statements by France as to its intended future conduct. A formal decision might have been divisive within the Court and therefore detrimental to its functioning. *Per contra* see comment by Schwebel, above n. 1, at 418, on these cases and on that of the Pakistani Prisoners of War, as to which see the Order of December 15, 1973 I.C.J. 347.

14 *See* 1. *Correspondence*, 84 Am. J. Int'l L. 231-3 (1990), following comment on the Nicaragua Case (below n. 16) that had referred to the background of some of the judges involved; 2. *Letter*, N. Y. Times, July 26, 1986 (reprinted McWhinney, above n. 12, at 109-111); 3. Manfred Lachs, *Some Reflections on the Nationality of Judges of the International Court of Justice*, 4 Pace Y.B. Int'l. L. 49-68 (1992).

15 North Sea Continental Shelf Cases, (Germany v. Netherlands; Germany v. Denmark) Judgement, 1969 I.C.J. Rep. 3 (February 20), Diss. Op. Lachs J., 219; Application for Review of Judgement No. 273 of the United Nations Administrative Tribunal, Advisory Opinion, [the "Mortished" case] 1982 I.C.J. 325 (July 20), Diss. Op. Lachs J., 411.

16 E.g. Barcelona Traction, Light and Power Company, Limited, 1970 I.C.J. 3 (February 5), Declaration of Lachs J. at 52-3; Case concerning United States Diplomatic and Consular Staff in Tehran, 1980 I.C.J. 3 (May 20), Sep. Op. Lachs J. at 47; Case concerning Military and Paramilitary Activities in and against Nicaragua, Merits, 1986 I.C.J. 14 (June 27), Sep. Op. Lachs J. at 158; Application for Review of Judgement No. 333 of the UN Administrative Tribunal, Advisory Opinion, 1987 I.C.J. 18 (May 28), Declaration of Lachs J. at 74.

majorities.[17] His ability to persuade and to assemble consensus in the greater interest was thereby protected.[18]

Throughout Lachs expounded and was persuasive of an activist approach to international law. His already mentioned linguistic facility meant that he was able to draw on writings in many languages, giving him a broad base of knowledge of world attitudes from which to develop his ideas – a base which those of us restricted to one or two languages lack. He showed that international law is not to be considered as the same as domestic law where legislation and domestic cases set parameters. Rather international law is a dynamic system operated for the most part by the legal advisers of state and other government departments in their international relations and by their cognates in international organisations. Only occasionally is recourse to judicial decision required, but, when it is, international law could not stand aside from the great issues of the day. In particular technological advance clearly posed problems that had to be coped with.[19] The very swiftness of that advance made it imperative that the law should itself move swiftly lest it become out of touch with the society it governs. Of course the major law-making process of international law is treaty, but treaty-making can often be slow and cumbrous. International custom might provide an alternative though again time could prove a hurdle. Lachs sought to argue that that hurdle might in appropriate instances be lowered. Thus his Dissent in the North Sea Continental Shelf Cases discusses the time element in the formation of international custom, noting that:

17 McWhinney, above n. 12, 18. At 17 McWhinney observes that it was during the Lachs Presidency that three major politically sensitive cases were decided, the Nuclear Test Cases, Australia v. France, 1974 I.C.J. 253 (December 20), New Zealand v. France, 1974 I.C.J. 457 (December 20), and the Western Sahara Case, 1975 I.C.J. 12 (October 16). In these Lachs was influential in the Court's producing a decision on a clear reasoned basis.

18 Higgins, above n. 1, states that advocates before the Court believed it necessary to carry Lachs with them because his views nearly always represented the majority.

19 Manfred Lachs, *Views from the Bench: Thoughts on Science, Technology and World Law*, 86 Am. J. Int'l L. 673-699 (1992); Manfred Lachs, *Some Reflections on the State of the Law of Outer Space*, 9 J. Space Law 3-11 (1981).

> ... the great acceleration of social and economic change, combined with that of science and technology, have confronted law with a serious challenge: one it must meet, lest it lag even farther behind events than it has been wont to do.[20]

Part III of the Dissent therefore set out how the views, attitudes and practical measures taken by states, could, apart from formal statement, show an emergent underlying generality of response to new problems that might help guide the Court. And, immediately following on the above quotation, Lachs cited the emerging law of space as a clear example of what could be done along those lines.

For Lachs the law should be developed rationally to deal with emergent problems, but developed through consensus and persuasion. This approach underlies his delivery of *The Development and General Trends of International Law in Our Time*, the 1980 General Course at The Hague.[21] In its extensive references Lachs sought to show through the citation of many legal traditions and materials that there was an underlying understanding of principle, which had to be understood in the interest of all. It was also important that a proper understanding of the nature and purpose of international law should be transmitted to those who would come after.

The dissemination of international law has two aspects. First, one should remember that Art. 38.1.d of the ICJ Statute places the "teachings of the most highly qualified publicists of the various nations" as one of the "subsidiary means for the determination of rules of law." Teachings are important on that level, aiding the rational development of the law. Second, teachings are also important on the level of the instruction of newcomers, the students. Lachs' 1976 lectures on "Teachings and Teaching on International Law" make clear

20 North Sea Continental Shelf Cases, (Germany v. Netherlands; Germany v. Denmark) Judgement, 1969 I.C.J. 3 (February 20), Diss. Op. Lachs, J, 219 at 231.

21 Manfred Lachs, The Development and General Trends of International Law in our Time, the General Course in Public International Law, 169 1980-IV *Receuil des Cours*, 9-337. A rather dismissive brief review by A.P. Rubin (79 Am. J. Int'l. L. 254-5 (1985)) is well met in the Lachs obituary by S.K. Chopra, above n. 1. That this General Course was not published commercially as a separate book is to be regretted.

the duty of those who teach the subject.[22] Elements of that exposition were further elaborated in the seminal *The Teacher in International Law* of 1982.[23] International law cannot be limited to abstract notions and the semantic nuances discerned by some academics, but must consider the political, economic, historical, financial, technological and social elements in the matters that require its services. Teachers of international law should be informed in many (perhaps all) such areas and so be able to base their teaching on a breadth of knowledge and thereby enthuse their students, fitting them to meet the requirements of the modern age.

In the course of spreading his views Lachs was an encouragement and encouraging to many, to those entering on the professional practice of international law, to those embarking on an academic career, and in particular to students.[24] His contributions while on the Court to The Hague Academy *Receuil des Cours* as well as other writings cited in this chapter show that he remained active in scholarship despite a heavy work-load. He also was busy with many lectures and invited addresses.[25] In all of these his wide-ranging references to classical, historical and technological parallels and cogent illustrations in text and footnote show a well-stocked, agile mind at work. The clarity of his writing and the felicities of its expression helped well to transmit his ideas.

22 Manfred Lachs, *Teachings and Teaching on International Law*, 151 1976-III *Receuil des Cours*, 161-252.

23 Manfred Lachs, The Teacher in International Law (Teachings and Teaching) (1982; 2d ed. 1986). The book was awarded the American Society of International Law prize for 1982. Cf. review by T.M. Franck, (1983) 77 Am. J. Int'l L. 169-170, who specifically comments on the felicity of its writing style; R.Y. Jennings, *Teachers and Teaching in International Law* in Mazarczyk, above n. 12, 121.

24 Thus during his term in the Court Lachs presided over the annual Telders International Moot Court Competition at The Hague, and, as President of the International Institute of Space Law, was behind the creation in 1992 of the space law moot court that now bears his name.

25 For bibliographies see McWhinney, above n. 12, and down to its date Mazarczyk, above n. 12, 18-23. The ICJ Obituary Notice indicates that Lachs was the recipient of nineteen honorary doctorates. It also lists his books and notes that he had published 145 articles in 11 languages: ICJ Communique 93/1, January 14, 1993.

In terms of space law the most important work and influence of Lachs is to a degree not formally recorded. The *procés verbaux* of A.AC.105 might be consulted, but his diligent consensus-seeking activities really remain only to be deduced. Much was done outwith the sessions of formal negotiations of COPUOS by way of individual and small-group conversation. Apart from the COPUOS involvement there are the two major expositions of space law to be reviewed.

"Need I apologise for my choice of subject?": with these words Lachs introduced his 1964 Hague lectures on space law.[26] He was well-placed to tackle the subject. Recognising the emergence of activities in space the UN had constituted the Committee on the Peaceful Uses of Outer Space (COPUOS) (A/AC.105) first, in 1958 as an *ad hoc* committee, and then a year later as a permanent committee.[27] The importance of this development was underlined by COPUOS being set up as separate rather than as a sub-set of any existing main committee. Within COPUOS itself two subcommittees were established. The Scientific and Technical Subcommittee was to ensure that COPUOS deliberations were informed by the best advice as to the facts. The function of the Legal Subcommittee was to consider the legal response to that knowledge and Lachs was elected as its first chairman. Real work started in 1962 and within eighteen months it was Lachs who, on behalf of the main committee, presented the *Declaration of Legal Principles Governing the Activities of States in the Exploration and Use of Outer Space* to the UN General Assembly on 13 December 1963. There the Declaration was adopted without vote.[28] Half a century later it is curious how modern space lawyers do not always recognise the extent of the achievement represented by that agree-

26 Manfred Lachs, *The International Law of Outer Space*, 113 1964-III, *Recueil des Cours*, 1–114.

27 *Question of the peaceful use of outer space*, U.N.G.A. Res. 1348 (XIII) 13 December 1958; *International cooperation in the peaceful uses of outer space*, U.N.G.A. Res. 1472 (XIV) 12 December 1959. Para 1.b of both Resolutions specifically called on the Committee to "study the nature of legal problems" arising from the exploration of outer space.

28 *Declaration of Legal Principles Governing the Activities of States in the Exploration and Use of Outer Space*, U.N.G.A. Res. 1962 (XVIII) December 13, 1963: 3 I.L.M. 157 (1964). Adoption without vote is the highest status possible for a U.N.G.A. Resolution.

ment on the Principles. Only months earlier the Cold War between East and West had been at an all-time high. The Cuba Missile Crisis of 1962 went close to armed conflict – perhaps even to nuclear war. Therefore, COPUOS having agreed that it would proceed by way of consensus, the role of the Chairman of the Legal Subcommittee in shepherding the negotiators and discussants towards agreement was crucial.[29] A later comment of Lachs on consensus reflects the difficulties he faced:

> Consensus is certainly a very painstaking process, it requires great patience and mutual understanding, particularly in an atmosphere of tension and distrust. However, while taxing the patience of delegates it turned out to be effective.[30]

Thereafter, we may be sure, Lachs was equally persuasive in the conversion of the 1963 Principles into the 1967 Outer Space Treaty,[31] which he was proud to present for approval to the Political Committee of the General Assembly on 16 December 1966.[32]

While a number of other books had by then been written on space law the simplicity of the 1964 Lectures is remarkable. The exposition is now mainly of historic importance, but they remain fascinating. In effect they take the reader through provisions of the 1963 Principles and make plain what had still to be done. The Introduction to the Lectures speaks of international law as a "wonderland of law" as it copes with the requirements of scientific and technological advance. Chapter I outlines "Man's Entry into Space" before going on to summarise past law-making processes, analogies from existing law,

29 COPUOS Verbatim Record, Second Meeting, Mar. 19 1962, UN Doc. A/AC.105/PV 2, 5, quoted by Lachs, above n. 26, 30 n.13. It should also be noted that the process was aided by many of the participants in the discussions being friends, anxious that space should be regulated on a generally agreed basis, political difference notwithstanding.

30 Manfred Lachs, *The Treaty on the Principles of the Law of Outer Space, 1961–1992*, 39 Neth. Int'l L. Rev. 291–302, 293 (1992).

31 Treaty on Principles Governing the Activities of States in the Exploration and Use of Outer Space Including the Moon and Other Celestial Bodies, London, Moscow and Washington, January 27, 1967, 610 U.N.T.S. 205 (1968). Cf. Lachs, above n. 30.

32 Manfred Lachs, below n. 39, at 128.

and the difficulties of law-making for space. Chapter II turns to the first attempts to formulate principles for outer space, including the definition of the subject of the new law, what we now know as the boundary question, and the application of international law to outer space. Chapter III then introduces substantive law, the "no national appropriation" principle, the legal status of objects launched into space, their definition, jurisdiction and ownership, the position of astronauts and their assistance, and the return of space objects. Chapter IV covers the rights of states in outer space, pointing out that while the exploration and use of space is free for all states, in fact, as new principles and rules develop, the freedom of action of states is increasingly reduced. Lachs summarises the obligations and responsibilities involved, including an interesting discussion of questions of liability that makes it clear that principles of liability needed first to be established and then, for effectiveness, translated into treaty form. The final lecture, Chapter V, moves into three specific areas of the use of space, telecommunications, and the tension between peaceful uses and arms and armaments in outer space, before concluding with some thoughts on the future.

Much of the content of the 1964 lectures on Space Law has been overtaken by later developments. However, before we pass from them mention should be made of a few pages in the middle of Chapter V, pages 95-99.[33] These foreshadow the argument of Lach's first dissent on the Court. The underlying question is the speed of technical developments, the emergence of new problems and the need for the law to respond. The processes of traditional law-making were having difficulty in keeping up. In these pages Lachs took up the question of the effect of resolutions of the UN General Assembly. While acknowledging the traditional legal position that UN resolutions are (with limited exception[34]) only recommendations, he doubted whether it would be accurate to deny them of all legal value. In many instances resolutions have paved "the way to new principles and rules of law, which in due course take the shape of binding international instruments. They initiate the law-making process by taking us across the threshold into the realms of law. Sometimes they may even create law, imperfect as it may be." He then turned to the 1963

33 M. Lachs, above n. 26, 95-99, footnotes omitted hereafter.

34 General Assembly resolutions regarding the UN conditions of service and other personnel matters do make law.

Declaration of Legal Principles, drawing attention in particular to several elements that they possess. First, the interpretation of the Principles by UN members, and particularly by those playing a leading part in the exploration and use of space, was important. The U.S. and U.S.S.R. had stated their intention to respect the Principles. Many other UN members had made similar statements. Thus, while there might some divergence as to interpretation:

> ... it can be said that almost all Members of the United Nations attached to [the Declaration] an importance similar to that resulting from a legally binding instrument, assimilating it, as it were, to the latter.
>
> Thus, by expressing their willingness to be bound by the provisions of the document in question, they consented so to be bound, and there is no reason why they should not be held to it, for their intention seems to be clear – the question of form ceases to be of essence.[35]

Second, the Principles had been preceded by other UN Resolutions, which though less explicit and limited in scope, "reflected a trend of development of the law *in statu nascendi*."[36] Third, practice, including practice prior to the adoption of the Declaration, had already conformed to certain of the Principles. Although some might argue that non-space-active states had merely acquiesced in the activities of the few, Lachs considered that their expressed attitudes evidenced a general consent (*tacitus consensus*), a more active thing than acquiescence. As for the question of the passage of time in the possible creation of custom, he observed that: "today time travels much faster and makes institutions mature at a much quicker speed than ever before."[37] Based on these points Lachs concluded that the "great value and strength [of the Declaration] is that it has created a framework for the law of tomorrow." The final pages of Chapter V make the case for the development of that law. Lacunae had to be filled. The "benefit and interests of all mankind" had to be

35 Lachs, above n. 26, at 98. Cf. his *Some Reflections on Substance and Form in International Law* in TRANSNATIONAL LAW IN A CHANGING SOCIETY: ESSAYS IN HONOR OF PHILIP C. JESSUP, 99-112 (Wolfgang Friedmann et al. eds,1972).

36 Lachs cited in particular U.N.G.A. Resolutions 1721 (XVI), December 20, 1961 and 1802 (XVIII), December 14, 1962.

37 M. Lachs, above n. 26, at 99; cf. Lachs, below n. 39, at 127-8.

secured in many aspects as space law was elaborated. A wide interpretation should be given to existing law in order to limit and exclude any tendency to exclusivism and unilateral action on the part of the space-active states. The rights of those as yet unable to benefit from space applications should be secured. As to process, the best recourse would be the gradual extension of principles and then their incorporation in treaty. In this lawmakers should work in two directions, from principle to detail and from detail to principle. Work on particular areas of concern such as rescue and return of astronauts, and on liability for damage was already under way.

The trouble with The Hague *Receuil des Cours* is that it is published as a series which not many law-school libraries can afford to take (or maintain). While an invitation to deliver lectures at the Academy is highly prized by its recipient, the content of the lectures is not, therefore, as widely available or as publicised as would in most cases be desirable.[38] It was therefore good that in 1972 Lachs published *The Law of Outer Space: An Experience in Contemporary Law-Making*.[39] Its commercial availability was to be welcomed. In effect this book is a second edition of the 1964 lectures, taking account of developments in the interim.

The Law of Outer Space is a slender book compared with its contemporaries in the field. As with the 1964 Lectures, some of it has become history, but its percipience cannot be denied. In an Introduction, twelve brief chapters and a Conclusion it covers most of what remain the major elements of the public international law of space. Each has fascinating references drawn from a wide set of sourcing.[40] Account is taken of the 1967 Outer Space Treaty, the 1968 Agreement on Rescue and Return and the 1972 Liability Convention. The Registration Convention of 1976 and Moon Agreement of 1979, of course,

38 Since this was written HeinOnline has made the Hague Academy *Receuil des Cours* available to those who include it in their subscription to that service.

39 Manfred Lachs, The Law of Outer Space: An Experience in Contemporary Law-Making (1972), republished on the occasion of the 50th anniversary of the International Institute of Space Law, T. Masson-Swaan & S. Hobe, eds. (2010).

40 These include Janáček, H.G. Wells, Jules Verne and Edgar Allen Poe, letters to The Times (of London), Joliot-Curie's Nobel Prize speech, and a wide range of scholarly discussion. However, more valuable may be the reproduction of materials otherwise buried in official documentation.

lay in the future. From the standpoint of 2012 there is but one lack. Although Lachs worked with public international law, one wonders what he would have made of the extension of private enterprise into space.

In his Foreword Lachs stated his intention. It was to provide a brief account of the first developments of space law and to indicate trends, others having already taken on the burden of detail. He felt that such a summary would be useful. He also suggested that the experience of law-making for space could be both illustrative and cautionary for those engaged in other areas where development was similarly swift. An Introduction then sweeps through the history of space including what had recently occurred, as well as its artistic and novelistic depictions. Access to space had allowed swift telecommunications and remote sensing which could be beneficial, yet that access was also causing apprehension as to state security. International co-operation would be needed and state conduct "must be submitted to the rule of law". The text would provide a short account of what had been done in that regard.

Chapter I shows how space law is a new horizon for international law. There Lachs makes a compelling argument that the setting of and agreement on general principles could form obligations binding *erga omnes*, that is binding even on non-parties to the formal instruments containing those principles. Chapter II turns to the new chapter of international law that space forms. Faced with a novel problem lawyers tend to transplant concepts from areas of known law. Lachs accepts that this can be a valid method of legal development, but warns that law-making by analogy is not always helpful. In particular analogies drawn from the law of the sea or air law and applied to questions of space might mislead. Space law should look forward, not back, and should be informed by the entire corpus of international law as it is most recently understood. That said, his Chapter III outlines the first stages of international cooperation in the development of space law, cooperation being both formal between states and through discussions in COPUOS as well as by the activities of such as the International Astronautical Federation. He stresses, no doubt from experience, the difficulties of tackling the "complex and laborious" process of matching science and technological progress with "modest yet important progress" in law.

Lachs then takes up particular areas of space law. Chapter IV considers outer space and celestial bodies. Reading the chapter now triggers questions as to the possible relationship between property rights and a lack of sovereignty. We may yet see a revision of the 1979 Moon Agreement or some other solution as the entrepreneurs come on the scene. Chapter V turns to the delimitation of space, both its inner and outer frontiers. No solution to the boundary question is offered, though Lachs notes that in the future some sort of "innocent passage" through foreign airspace may be required for states exercising their freedom to use outer space. In Chapter VI Lachs considers the legal situation of objects launched into outer space and of astronauts, while Chapter VII more directly reviews the 1968 Agreement on Rescue and Return of both objects and of astronauts. Space Telecommunications are the brief subject of Chapter VIII, though it may be noted that the content of telecommunications by way of propaganda registers as a substantial matter of concern. Chapter IX then deals with arms and armament and the "peaceful use" requirements of space law. General progress towards disarmament is seen as necessary. Chapter X covers the rights and responsibilities of states, making it clear that cooperation and sharing of benefit is fostered by the principles of space law in a manner not found in earlier international law. Chapter XI more detailedly discusses questions of state responsibility, pointing out that the extension of human activity into the new medium has extended both the rights and the duties of states. The conditions that make a state responsible have been set both in the Outer Space Treaty and in the Liability Convention. There has been great innovation here. Normally a state is responsible only for its own illicit act. Space law makes a state liable also for the acts of its nationals, and in some instances that liability is absolute.

Following the material of its predecessors, Chapter XII on the law-making process is compelling. The progress from principle to treaty is sketched. "The process was not an easy one" (p. 129) is an illuminating comment from one who was heavily involved until called to other things. Importantly Lachs notes (p. 130) that the record shows that it was not just the space-active states that made the running. Many other non-space-active states contributed with constructive proposals, many of which are now in the final instruments.

Last there are the Conclusions. In two pages Lachs reaffirms the need for scientific and technical advance to be understood, and for lawyers to be constantly mindful of the need to change, adapt and develop law suitable to contain these new achievements. He points to the environmental degradation that can accompany industrial processes exploiting new technologies, and affirms that law could provide solutions. Rules of conduct, of restraint and prohibition, as well as measures of cooperation and conscious moderation in the interests of all, these can all be seen at work space law. Its successes, as well as its imperfections, provide a model of how international law can (and implicitly must) be developed to meet modern requirements.

The life and work of Manfred Lachs cannot here be briefly summed up, let alone his significance within the relatively restricted sphere of space law. We should be grateful that space law took his attention as an area in which international law had to progress with unwonted swiftness. He saw the utility of the route from principle to law and was persuasive of it. His writings show the breadth of knowledge that lay behind that realisation. His skill in achieving cooperation in the development of space law cannot be denied. His influence on so many of us is clear. Perhaps the best conclusion to be made is therefore simply to quote the final sentences of those 1964 lectures on "The International Law of Outer Space":

> The path has been mapped. All I intended to do was to report to you the achievements of today and to indicate the way into tomorrow.[41]

The words of a pioneer indeed.

41 Manfred Lachs, above n. 26, at 103.

Bibliography

THE INTERNATIONAL LAW OF OUTER SPACE, 113 1964-III *Recueil des Cours*, (The Hague Academy of International Law), 1–114.

THE LAW OF OUTER SPACE: AN EXPERIENCE IN CONTEMPORARY LAW-MAKING (Leiden: Sijthoff, 1972: rep. T. Masson-Swaan and S. Hobe, eds. (Leiden and Boston: Nijhoff, 2010)).

Teachings and Teaching on International Law, 151 1976-III *Receuil des Cours*, 161-252.

The Development and General Trends of International Law in Our Time, the Hague Academy of International Law, General Course in Public International Law, 169 1980-IV *Receuil des Cours*, 9-337.

Some Reflections on the State of the Law of Outer Space, 9 J. SPACE LAW, 3-11, (1981).

THE TEACHER IN INTERNATIONAL LAW (TEACHINGS AND TEACHING) (The Hague: Nijhoff, 1982; 2d ed. 1986).

Views from the Bench: Thoughts on Science, Technology and World Law, 86 AM. J. INT'L L. 673-699 (1992).

The Treaty on the Principles of the Law of Outer Space 1961–1992, 39 NETH. INT'L. L. REV. 291–302 (1992).

About the International Institute of Space Law

Founded in 1960, the International Institute of Space Law (IISL) is an independent non-governmental organisation dedicated to fostering the development of space law. The membership of the Institute is composed of individuals and institutions from more than forty countries elected on the basis of their contributions to the field of space law or other social sciences related to space activities. In addition, prospective membership is open to students and young professionals with a demonstrated interest in space law.

The purposes and objectives of the IISL include the promotion of further development of space law and expansion of the rule of law in the exploration and use of outer space for peaceful purposes, the holding of meetings, colloquia and competitions on juridical and social science aspects of space activities, the preparation or commissioning of studies and reports, the publication of books, proceedings, reports and position papers, and the cooperation with appropriate international organizations and national institutions in the field of space law.

The IISL holds an annual Colloquium at the International Astronautical Congress. During this Colloquium the Nandasiri Jasentuliyana Keynote lecture takes place, as well as a special session for Young Scholars. In addition the Institute organises a variety of conferences on space law throughout the year in locations all over the world. It publishes an annual volume of IISL Proceedings with papers and reports of all activities during the year.

Since 1992, the IISL organizes the annual Manfred Lachs Space Law Moot Court Competition. The competition is based on a hypothetical space law case, written by IISL members, in which around sixty student teams from universities in North America, Europe, Asia Pacific and Africa participate. Members of the International Court of Justice judge the World Finals of the competition, making it unique in the world.

The IISL is an officially recognized observer at sessions of the United Nations Committee on the Peaceful Uses of Outer Space, and its Scientific & Technical and Legal Subcommittees. In cooperation with the European Centre for Space Law (ECSL), the IISL organizes an annual space law symposium for the delegates and staff attending the sessions of the UNCOPUOS Legal Subcommittee.

Further information regarding the IISL can be found at www.iislweb.org.

www.ingramcontent.com/pod-product-compliance
Lightning Source LLC
LaVergne TN
LVHW081515300926
849161LV00006B/1189
* 9 7 8 9 0 0 4 2 4 0 2 7 8 *